The
Power Wish

life

Keiko is Japan's leading astrologer and manifestation expert. Her mission is to help people around the world create the life they have always wanted. She is the founder of Lunalogy, a groundbreaking method for attracting fortune using the energy and the cycle of the Moon, and is the creator of an original manifestation technique she calls Power Wish. She has written more than twenty books about Lunalogy and the Power Wish Method, selling more than one million copies in Japan. Her easy-to-follow techniques and relatable advice have attracted legions of fans, including many Japanese celebrities and political figures, who are drawn to her spiritual yet practical outlook. Keiko is now thrilled to bring—for the first time ever—the life-changing potential of Lunalogy and Power Wish to readers everywhere.

Visit Keiko online at keikopowerwish.com, and follow @keikopowerwish on Instagram.

Wish

The
Power Wish

JAPAN'S LEADING ASTROLOGER
REVEALS THE MOON'S SECRETS
FOR FINDING SUCCESS,
HAPPINESS, AND THE
FAVOR OF THE UNIVERSE

Keiko

*Translated from the Japanese
by Rieko Yamanaka*

PENGUIN LIFE

VIKING
An imprint of Penguin Random House LLC
penguinrandomhouse.com

Originally published in Japan as *Shingetsu Mangetsu No Power Wish: Keiko Teki Uchuu Ni Ekohiiki Sareru Negai No Kakikata* by Kodansha, Tokyo, in 2017.
Copyright © 2017 by Keiko Ariizumi.

Translation copyright © 2021 by Keiko Ariizumi

A Penguin Life Book

Images on pages 69, 83, 97, 111, 125, 139, 153, 167, 181, 195, 209, and 223 from ilusmedical/Shutterstock.com.
Image first appearing on page 60 designed by Freepik.
Illustrations on pages 256 and 265 by Nozomi Yuasa.

LIBRARY OF CONGRESS CATALOGING-IN-PUBLICATION DATA

Names: Keiko, author. | Yamanaka, Reiko, 1957– translator.
Title: The power wish : Japan's leading astrologer reveals the moon's secrets for finding success, happiness, and the favor of the universe / Keiko ; translated from Japanese by Rieko Yamanaka.
Other titles: Shingetsu mangetsu no pawā wisshu. English
Description: New York : Viking, 2021. | Originally published in Japan by Kodansha, 2017.
Identifiers: LCCN 2019052470 (print) | LCCN 2019052471 (ebook) |
ISBN 9781984880420 (hardcover) | ISBN 9781984880437 (ebook)
Subjects: LCSH: Astrology. | Moon—Miscellanea.
Classification: LCC BF1723 .K4513 2020 (print) | LCC BF1723 (ebook) |
DDC 133.5—dc23
LC record available at https://lccn.loc.gov/2019052470
LC ebook record available at https://lccn.loc.gov/2019052471

Printed in the United States of America
1 3 5 7 9 10 8 6 4 2

Designed by Meighan Cavanaugh

Contents

Part 2 · Harness the 12 Zodiac Signs' Areas of Expertise

Part 3 · Getting More Out of Your Power Wish

Introduction

Since ancient times, astrology has been one of the most reliable sources of wisdom available to mankind. I'm sure many of you have read books about astrology, or received astrology readings.

Perhaps to discover your unique talent and potential.

Perhaps to find out when your next big window of opportunity will come along.

Or perhaps to see how compatible you are with your beloved partner.

And yet . . .

Did the answer truly satisfy you?

Did your life really shift in the direction you desired?

Let me rephrase the question: What if you read in a book that you're going to be stuck in a huge slump for the next three years? What if you went to see an astrologer and were told that you and your partner have the worst compatibility possible, and that marrying them would ruin your life?

Neither of these scenarios can be solved using astrology as it stands now. Why? Because astrology itself isn't equipped to make your wishes come true.

There is, however, an exception: the Power Wish.

The Power Wish is neither a way of discovering yourself, nor a technique to predict the future. It doesn't matter who you are or what kind of star you were born under. The Power Wish is a method for making your wishes come true. And it uses the astrological system of the twelve zodiac signs for that purpose.

There are so many astrology fans out there, but unfortunately most of them know how to use it only in a rather passive manner. On the contrary, the Power Wish is a proactive method of applied astrology. (To me, this is actually the best part of astrology.) It's an extremely practical and effective way to rely on the great power of the Universe to create your dream life.

The Power Wish Method is the secret art of manifesting your heart's desires. It is a technique for making your dreams come true that has never before been taught.

A Power Wish is essentially a New Moon wish, a wish made when the Moon is in the New Moon phase of its monthly cycle—and yet it is so much more than that. The reason I call it a Power Wish is because this technique actually has enough power to move the Universe.

When you make a wish on the New Moon, it comes true—that's an indisputable fact. A New Moon occurs when the Moon perfectly overlaps the Sun. It corresponds to day zero in the Moon cycle, so if it were a human, it would be a newborn baby—which means all growth starts here.

When you plant the seed of a wish on the New Moon, it bears fruit. This isn't magic. As far as the cycle of the Universe is concerned, it's perfectly natural.

That said, you'll need to know a few tricks to harness this power of manifestation. Write your wish at a designated time using words of high vibration. That is the Ironclad rule of the Power Wish Method.

By using the Power Wish Method myself, I got into my first-choice college, got a job at the company I wanted to work for, struck out on my own at the perfect time, achieved instant success in multiple businesses of my own, received a miraculous offer to publish a book as a completely unknown author, and won the heart of the man I love. That's right—everything in my life goes my way!

This is all because I was covertly using Power Wishes the whole time. I alone knew the secret art—no one else did.

You don't need hard work to make your wishes come true. Talent has nothing to do with it, either. As a matter of fact, you don't even need to wish hard. The only requirement is to know the rules of the Power Wish Method. All you need to do is make your wish according to its rules.

PART I

What Is the New Moon and Full Moon Power Wish Method?

Whereas most astrologers read the flow of all things primarily through Sun signs, I use the Moon as my lens. This is the key difference between common astrology and my brand of astrology, which I call *Lunalogy*.

Lunalogy is a method for attracting good fortune through the Moon, and it consists of three elements:

1. Personal Moon Sign

Your personal Moon sign reflects your innate gravity—the power to attract things into your life. It is your Moon sign, not your Sun sign, that attracts all things that lead to happiness, such as career and romantic opportunities, true callings, sources of income, and soul mates. Why? Because of the Moon's gravitational pull.

My theory is that making the most out of your personal Moon sign is the key to finding good fortune and happiness.

For more details on personal Moon signs, see page 240 ("Technique 1: Take Full Advantage of the New Moon and Full Moon Occurring in Your Moon Sign").

2. Daily Moon Sign

The Moon moves through each of the twelve zodiac signs every two and a half days, completing a full cycle in approximately 29.5 days. When you know which sign the Moon is in on any given day and take appropriate action (in how you dress, eat, live, act, see, and think), you are in sync with the rhythm of the Universe, which will bring you good fortune. If you make a habit of living according to the daily Moon sign, you will naturally become successful.

3. Power Wish

The Power Wish is a manifestation method that fully utilizes both your innate gravity (personal Moon sign) and the Moon's gravity (daily Moon sign). It is an extremely precise way to manifest your wishes and dreams using the gravity of the Moon at its peak every month, on the New Moon and the Full Moon. In this book, I explain this method in detail.

Why Wishing on the Moon Works

The New Moon, which occurs every month, is the day when the Moon and the Sun are in perfect alignment. Many people have a practice of journaling about their dreams and wishes on this day, but do you know why wishes come true when you write them down on the New Moon?

The Moon is the Earth's only satellite, a presence that connects the Earth to the Universe. Imagine an "Earth help desk" that acts as a liaison between those of us living on the Earth and the other planets in the solar system. The Moon is our designated help desk, delivering our wishes to the Universe.

The Moon is not the only thing that works hard for you; strictly speaking, it's the Universe that manifests your wish. Still, given that the Moon has been serving as the Earth's help desk for more than two hundred million years, there's no doubt that the smoothest way to send wishes to the Universe is via the Moon.

The Moon is the Earth's agent

You know how various brands have authorized retailers that function as satellite "agents" for the brands? Through the local stores, we can order the item we want (make a wish), and then receive that item (wish comes true). Wishing on the Moon works because it follows the same process. The Moon is the Earth's "agent," delivering wishes to the Universe.

It's important to note, however, that timing is key. Why? Because the Universe is not accepting orders 24/7. Just as stores have operating hours, the Universe also restricts the days it accepts wishes from us—to just two.

What determines whether your wish comes true?

The New Moon and the Full Moon are the two days every month that the Universe has designated for accepting our wishes. The reason that wishes on the New Moon and Full Moon tend to come true is that the Universe is already willing to grant them. As a general principle, the Universe intends to fulfill wishes it receives on the New and Full Moons.

If your wishes aren't coming true even though you made them on the right days, you need to realize that the problem lies with you. It means that you don't know how to effectively write your wishes.

Think about it: If you apply for a job, your application is first screened by the person in charge. If they don't approve of it, it's game over—in other words, your wish won't come true. This being the case, if you want your wish to come true, you need to write an application that grabs the heart of the one in charge.

In other words, in order to have your wish come true, you need to write it in such a way that it draws the Universe in. Even better is if it wins the Universe's favor so that you can become its favorite! That's right: Whether your wish comes true depends on *how* you write it.

If Your New Moon Wish Hasn't Come True

Every time I update my Japanese blog on the New Moon, I receive the same request from my readers: "Please teach me how to wish on the New Moon. If you have your own special writing method, I'd really like to know."

Although my readers have been asking this for a while, I had put it on the back burner, thinking it wasn't that urgent.

However, just recently I received this email from Chikako, one of my readers:

"I've been writing my wishes on the New Moon for more than three years, ever since I heard it's helpful. Although some of them have come true, the vast majority of them have not. Why is that? Am I writing them wrong? Or is there something fundamentally wrong with me?"

The trick is to get the Universe "in the mood"

"This is how I usually write my wishes," Chikako continued. "If I'm writing them wrong, could you give me advice on how to write them properly?"

As I read the wishes she said she had written the previous month, I was struck by how different her style was from my own, in terms of both structure and word choice.

And I thought, "Hmm . . . would these words ever get the Universe in the mood to grant her wish?"

The Universe is the one with the power to grant your wish. So unless you write your wish in a way that gets the Universe in the mood, it's all for nothing, isn't it?

That's when I thought of my friend Ken, who is currently the HR manager for a major corporation. When I met him for drinks recently, he got a little tipsy and blurted out, "I hate to say this, but I never look through every single job application. There's never enough time for that; I get thousands of them at once. Instead, I quickly pick out the ones that shine, and only look at those. There are certain ones that catch my eye, you know?"

As I remembered Ken's words, it occurred to me that Chikako's wishes haven't caught the Universe's eye.

Furthermore, I realized that there must be many more people like Chikako who are writing wishes in a way that doesn't get the Universe's attention.

And if all those people are feeling sad that their wishes haven't come true, there's no way I can ignore them. I have to teach them how to write their wishes properly so that they actually reach the Universe. That is the reason I decided to write this book.

Merely writing your wishes won't do

A disclaimer before I begin: There is no such thing as a "correct" way to write a New Moon wish. There's no right or wrong way when it comes to writing wishes.

That being said, there's definitely an effective way—one that gets the Universe on your side.

That very method is what I'm about to share with you. With this method, you will not only catch the Universe's eye but also win its favor.

If there were a company you really wanted to work for, wouldn't you tailor your job application to appeal to it? How talented or motivated you are is not the most important thing; your application has to catch the hiring manager's attention first and foremost.

One more thing: Even if your application does catch their attention, if what you offer doesn't match their needs, it's pointless. If the company is looking for a salesperson, then showing off your talent and experience in accounting isn't going to get you hired, is it?

No matter how much effort you put into writing your job application, if it doesn't match the company's needs or catch the hiring manager's eye, chances are you won't get past the initial screening. Your aspiration to work for the company will go unfulfilled.

It's the same thing with New Moon wishes.

The "sweet spot" that grabs the Universe's attention

When you write your New Moon wishes, if all you do is make a laundry list of what you want, you'll never see results. It's the Universe that has the power to grant your wish, so you have to adapt the wish to its liking. Otherwise, there's no point in writing the wish to begin with.

If, however, you write your wishes in such a way that the Universe takes notice, then you're in the driver's seat. As my friend Ken said, there's a certain writing style that shines. It's like a "sweet spot" that puts the Universe in the mood.

If you hit that sweet spot with the writing of your wishes, then manifesting becomes a piece of cake. As you get the hang of it, you'll become so in tune with the Universe that it will feel as natural as breathing for your wishes to come true. Eventually, you'll reach a state in which they come true before you even make them. This all becomes possible when you get on the same wavelength as the Universe.

The conditions for winning the Universe's favor

Just so you know, the Universe isn't fair. Perhaps the Buddha or bodhisattvas would save everyone equally, but not the Universe. It's partial only to the people it likes—those who can keep up with its rhythm.

Do you think that's horrible?

But you see, the Universe has very good reasons for favoring certain people. It favors those who bring happiness to those around them, those who give generously, and those who have a positive influence on the world. Naturally, these people's wishes are prioritized by the Universe, because when the Universe manifests the wishes of those who have a positive impact on those around them, then more and more people can find happiness.

If you had to choose between granting the wishes of someone who cares about only what they want and granting those of someone else who is willing to share the joy, wealth, and happiness of their manifestation with many more people—well, which would you choose?

I bet it's the latter. The Universe feels the same way.

When the wish comes true, return the love and gratitude

The Universe's will is for the Earth to be filled with love and for every person living on it to find happiness. But the Universe can't do all this on its own. We, the inhabitants of the Earth, have to do our part.

This doesn't mean, however, that you have to devote your whole life to serving others. It's not as if the Universe is expecting us all to become like Mother Teresa. As humans, it's natural for us to go after our dreams and ideals and to want to enjoy life. Having desires is not a problem at all.

That said, you have to first understand that it's all thanks to the people around you—and their material and moral support—that your wish can come true. The Universe gives the direction, but other people are the ones who actually make your wish come true.

When your wish comes true, express your gratitude with love, and return your happiness to the world. If you continue this cycle for the rest of your life, there'll be no limit to the quantity and scale of wishes the Universe grants you.

The Keiko-Style New Moon and Full Moon Power Wish Method

The wish-making method I am about to introduce is one that, until writing this book, I have shared with only close friends. Before I begin, let me be clear about one thing: I don't call these wishes mere New (or Full) Moon wishes; instead I use the term *Power Wish*.

Wish vs. Power Wish

It's been a long time since I started calling it a Power Wish instead of just a wish. It bothered me that the vibration of the word *wish* felt a bit weak; it just didn't feel like a good-enough match for the incredible power of the New Moon and Full Moon. When I asked myself what to call it instead, Power Wish immediately came to mind.

You won't believe how many of my close friends started to make great progress in their manifestations as soon as I told them to call it a Power Wish instead of just a wish. And all they did was use a different term.

Yet this makes perfect sense, because words carry vibrations. Whether you're calling something by a new name or writing a wish, what's important is the vibration. Using words of the highest, most powerful vibration is the key to manifesting.

That's why I call it the Power Wish Method. It's an amazingly powerful way to make your dreams come true. Think of it as a way of bringing your heart's desires into reality, far beyond just wishing and hoping.

Power Wish examples

What goes into a Power Wish? How is it different from normal wish writing?

Before I get into the details, I'd like you to see some examples. One is a Power Wish I myself wrote recently. Another is one that my friend Wakako wrote.

Power Wish Example 1

For more than a year, I had been looking for a food manufacturer to create a new product.

Perhaps because my requirements were so strict, I hadn't been able to find a good one. "I guess it's not easy after all," I thought, almost ready to give up. But then I realized that the following day was the New Moon. "Wait a minute—this is the perfect time for a Power Wish!"

The New Moon was in Pisces. The strengths of Pisces are unconditional love and connection to the invisible, so Pisces is not really suited for business wishes. However, with the Power Wish Method, that's not an issue at all, because you can communicate with the Universe through special words I call **Anchoring Statements** and <u>Anchorings</u>. (I explain Anchoring Statements and Anchorings in more detail on page 36.)

This is the Power Wish I wrote at the time, word for word:

I am certain that the wish I am making is perfectly aligned with the will of the Universe, and that it is the highest and best way to bring love and prosperity into the world. Through the wish I am making, I intend for my love and power to quickly reach all beings everywhere.

Currently I am planning on developing a new product. <u>I intend to</u> find the best manufacturer to help me bring it to life and create a product filled with the vibration of love.

Furthermore, <u>I intend for</u> love to reach all those who receive my product, blessing them and their families with happiness.

One of the rules of the Power Wish Method is to write wishes not only on the New Moon, but also on the Full Moon (although the writing style is quite different). For Full Moon Power Wishes, you focus on gratitude and write them as though the wish has already come true. (I explain this in more detail on page 44.) Here's the Power Wish I wrote two weeks later, when the Full Moon was in Virgo:

I am grateful that my wish has been granted in the fastest way possible by the guidance of the Universe. I pledge to share this happiness with the world in every way that I can. I am grateful that the love and the light of the Universe are always with me.

I found a wonderful food manufacturer that meets my requirements perfectly and have entered into a contract with them. <u>I am so grateful for this miracle. Thank you so much!</u>

My idea has been so smoothly implemented, and the most perfect product has come to life. <u>I am blown away by the overwhelming responses from my customers! Thank you so much.</u>

These Power Wishes were written in late February, when the New Moon was in Pisces, and in mid-March, when the Full Moon was in Virgo. As soon as April came around, I got an email from my friend Osamu, whom I hadn't seen in a long time. "Wanna grab a drink this Thursday?" he wrote. "A friend of mine will be there, too."

When I arrived at our meeting spot that day, Osamu was with his friend Mr. Uchida, who, according to Osamu, was "just a drinking buddy." However, as we started talking, I found out that he was the CEO of a food manufacturing company! And when I described to him the product I wanted to make and how I hadn't been able to find a manufacturer, he said, "My company can totally do that. It's easy."

Osamu had no idea I was looking for a food manufacturer. Just by using the Power Wish Method, I was easily able to find the ideal manufacturer, despite having been unable to for more than a year.

Power Wish Example 2

When I saw my friend Wakako awhile back, she told me, "I'm interested in someone at work, but there hasn't been any progress. I don't really want to be the one to make a move, but he's not going to ask me out if I just wait around. I wonder if I should just give up."

To be honest, while listening to her, I was thinking, "This probably isn't going to work out." However, in three days the Full Moon was going to enter Aquarius, and two weeks after that, there was going to be a solar eclipse in Virgo. The timing couldn't have been more perfect.

A solar eclipse is sometimes said to be a special version of a New Moon. It's an astoundingly powerful time when your intentions can hold even more meaning than usual. Because of that timing, I had a feeling that my friend might be able to turn things around. So I asked her, "Hey, Wakako, would you like to try a thing called a Power Wish?"

And she responded enthusiastically, "Yes! Yes! Absolutely!"

Here's the Aquarius Full Moon Power Wish that Wakako wrote:

I am grateful that my wish has been granted in the fastest way possible by the guidance of the Universe. I pledge to share this happiness with the world in every way that I can. I am grateful that the love and the light of the Universe are always with me.

Fumito and I now go out all the time as if we're best friends. I couldn't be happier! Thank you so much.

Fumito and I are building a free and intellectually stimulating relationship in which we share a deep connection without needing to control each other. I'm feeling so fulfilled right now. Thank you so much.

Two of the key concepts of Aquarius are *friendship* and *freedom*. Even though it was her first Power Wish, Wakako did such a great job writing it, even incorporating these words—beautiful!

And here's the Power Wish that she wrote two weeks later, during the Virgo New Moon (a solar eclipse):

> I am certain that the wish I am making is per-
> fectly aligned with the will of the Universe, and
> that it is the highest and best way to bring love and
> prosperity into the world. Through the wish I am
> making, I intend for my love and power to quickly
> reach all beings everywhere.
>
> I intend to join the same gym as Fumito so that I
> can talk to him more often, winning his heart and
> getting into better shape at the same time.
>
> I intend to build a sincere relationship with Fumito
> and to provide ongoing support for him in his life.

Sincere and *support* are both keywords of Virgo. In addition, losing weight and shedding excess fat are signature
moves of the Virgo New Moon. When you write your wish
in a way that ties into the zodiac sign's area of expertise, the
chance of the wish coming true increases dramatically.

Visualizing to speed things up

There was one more thing I asked Wakako to do.

When you write a Power Wish, I strongly encourage you to incorporate visualization. Whereas a Power Wish is a way to place an order with the Universe through words, visualization does this through imagery. If you went to a hairstylist and said, "Please trim an inch off the back and add layers to the sides," they'd probably ask you to show them a photo of what that looks like. This is because having both words and images really clarifies things; it helps the stylist fulfill your request. The same goes for the Universe. When you add visualization to your Power Wish, the Universe can make it come true more quickly and accurately. This is exactly why visualizing while writing your wishes speeds up the manifestation process. Even if it's a pretty big wish, it's not unusual for it to present itself in just a few days.

When I suggested this to Wakako, she replied, "I'm terrible at visualizing." So what I had her do instead was cut out photos from magazines. By using images from magazines and the internet, even those who are not good mental visualizers can reap the benefits.

I asked Wakako to write her Power Wish on one page of a notebook, and on the facing page to make a collage of inspiring images that represented the kind of relationship she wanted with Fumito. And then I asked her to review it again when Mercury went into retrograde (see page 249 for details on this). With these simple steps, the effect of the words and images dramatically boosts the chance of the wish manifesting. It's as if the visuals breathe life into the Power Wish.

Personal Moon sign Power Wishes are amazingly powerful!

So Wakako gave her first Power Wish a try. What happened after that?

Four months later, one of Fumito's classmates joined Wakako's department, which quickly brought Fumito and Wakako close together. They began to go out, and currently they are thinking about marriage. According to Wakako, "This is all thanks to the Power Wish Method. Seriously."

It wasn't until later that I found out Wakako's Moon sign is Virgo, which means that her Power Wish, which she made during the Virgo New Moon, was her personal Moon sign Power Wish. How could it not have come true? (See page 65 for more on personal Moon sign Power Wishes.)

There you have it. Did you get a sense of what the Keiko-Style Power Wish Method is like? Now I'll explain it in more detail.

How to write a Power Wish

Power Wish Rule 1

Write your wishes as intentions on the New Moon;
write them as statements of gratitude on
the Full Moon.

The New Moon and the Full Moon make a pair
The basic principle of the Power Wish Method is to use the energies of both the New Moon and the Full Moon. Many people who regularly wish on the New Moon seem to just

make their wish and leave it—and that really is a job half-done. Not to mention, it's such a waste! Full Moons are just as powerful as New Moons, if not more.

On both the New Moon and the Full Moon, a high-quality communication channel opens up between the Earth and the Universe. It's like the Universe's Wi-Fi signal is flying all over the Earth. Because the signal is everywhere, it makes it easy for the Moon to receive your wish, fast and clear. If such an ideal opportunity regularly occurs twice a month, don't you think it's a waste to take advantage of only one of them?

The New Moon and the Full Moon have always been a natural pair. Although there are exceptions, the basic cycle of growth in nature is that the seeds you plant on the New Moon bear fruit on the Full Moon, and then on the following New Moon, the dispersed seeds plant themselves and bear fruit again on the Full Moon.

Any process of development and accomplishment requires the energies of both the New Moon and the Full Moon.

The same goes for wishes. If you make a wish on the New Moon and abandon it, you're not tending to the seed you planted. The buds that could have sprouted won't emerge. If you take the time to plant seeds, you also have to water them. Practicing gratitude on the Full Moon is the equivalent of watering your seeds.

Be aware, however, that the Full Moon is not the time to make a wish. The Full Moon is a time to give thanks for what you have received, even if you haven't received it yet. The Japanese Moon-viewing ceremony every fall takes place on the Full Moon in order to express gratitude for a rich harvest. There is a long tradition of practicing gratitude during the Full Moon.

The Full Moon is a time for gratitude

Perhaps you are thinking, "How can I be grateful when none of my wishes have come true?" If that's the case, you need to change your perspective. What's important here is not whether your wishes have come true. First, be grateful for what you have now. The key is to thank the Universe in advance, because it is about to grant you your wish. You don't thank it because your wishes have come true; your wishes come true *because* you thanked it. Gratitude comes first!

If you want water, you hold out a glass. If you want something, you first have to offer something.

Gratitude is offering the love and feelings from your heart. It's synonymous with giving love. When you offer gratitude, the Universe offers you love in return—that's what's happening when your wishes come true.

The balance between the New Moon and the Full Moon makes the wish come true

I want this, I want that, I want to do this, I want to be like this. . . . There are no limits to human desires. It's wonderful to have hopes and dreams, for they are what we live for, but if all you do is ask for what you want over and over again, doesn't it seem like something is missing?

The key to manifesting is *balance*. It's hard to realize this, but balance is crucial, because the whole world is made up of the balance between the yin and the yang.

There's the Moon and the Sun, and there's night and day. Man and woman, front and back, right and left, winter and summer . . . What governs this world is the balance of two opposites. If we had only the Moon or only night, the Earth itself couldn't exist, and of course we couldn't survive, either. It takes both the yin and the yang to make something happen.

The same goes for wishing. If all you do is ask for what you want, there's no balance. If there's no balance, things can't happen—in other words, your wish can't come true.

If you want your wishes to come true, you have to add the power of the opposite. That's what gratitude does. So you make a wish on the New Moon, and express gratitude on the Full Moon—that's the flow. It's as natural as inhaling and exhaling.

Power Wish Rule 2

Note the "area of expertise" for each zodiac sign that the New Moon or the Full Moon is in.

The New Moon and the Full Moon cycle through the twelve signs of the zodiac
Did you know that the New Moon and the Full Moon occur in a different sign of the zodiac each month? For example, the New Moon could be in Leo in August, Virgo in

September, Libra in October, and so on. The same goes for the Full Moon. Both the New Moon and the Full Moon pass through the twelve signs over the course of the whole year.

This means that with every New Moon and Full Moon, the energies are different.

If it's hard for you to grasp the idea of differences in energy, think of it as differences in areas of expertise. Cancer is good at families and households; Capricorn, at jobs and careers. Physical health is the domain of Virgo, and romantic relationships and marriage are the areas of Libra. In the case of the twelve zodiac signs, the division of the areas of expertise is quite clear, so it's a basic principle of the Power Wish Method to write your wishes and expressions of gratitude according to each.

For example, let's say you want to get promoted to a store manager position. Although it's perfectly fine to make that wish when the New Moon is in Cancer, there are other signs that are experts at this type of wish—namely Capricorn, Leo, and Aries. So it's important that you make the same wish again when the New or Full Moon occurs in these signs as well. (Although it's certainly possible for your wish to come true after just one Power Wish!) Would you ever go see an ear, nose, and throat doctor when your stomach hurts? Wouldn't a gastroenterologist be a better choice? You've got to see the expert in the field. The same goes for wishing.

If it's a wish that you're feeling quite relaxed about—something you just think would be nice if it came true one day—then you don't need to worry so much about the signs. But if you are serious about making it come true, you must write your wish in a way that's appropriate for each sign's area of expertise. You've got to go to the expert on the matter.

The signs that the New Moon and the Full Moon occur in reflect the area of life that the Universe's energy is focusing on at that time. The Universe is pouring all of its resources into that particular area, so if you make a wish and express gratitude accordingly, manifesting is easy. Once your will is aligned with the will of the Universe, it's no longer your personal wish—it's part of the will of the Universe. At this point, there's no more need for you to hustle on your own.

Planting seeds in twelve fields

Some of you may be wondering, "Does this mean that if I want to get married, I can make a wish only when the

Moon is in Libra [which is in charge of marriages]? Just once a year?"

Rest assured, you can write any wish at any time. All you have to do is change the wording according to the sign. For example, let's say you want to get married. When the New Moon is in Aries, which is good at beginnings, you can wish for "the beginning of a new relationship that leads to marriage." When the New Moon is in Taurus, which is good at financial stability, you have the option of wishing "to meet a wealthy marriage partner." If you want "a partner to have fun conversations with," you can wish for that the following month, when the New Moon is in Gemini, which is good at communication.

Just because each sign has its own area of expertise doesn't mean that none of the wishes in other areas can come true when the Moon is in that sign. All you have to do is write your wish in a way that relates to the area.

You can approach the same wish from twelve different angles. Doing so is like planting seeds in twelve different fields. From the Aries field to the Pisces field, plant seeds on all twelve for good measure. Leave it to the Universe to decide which field the seeds will sprout from.

She turned the wish into a Power Wish,
and a soul mate appeared!

Let me tell you the story of my friend Yoshimi. At the time, she was divorced and wished to marry her soul mate within a year. Ever since she'd heard a friend mention that New Moon wishes come true, she had been making the same wish for more than a year. "I'm putting so much energy into writing my wish, so how come it's not coming true?" she wondered. By the time a year has passed, the New Moon has cycled through all twelve zodiac signs, which means that even if the wish hasn't completely come true, there should be some kind of shift or development. (Meeting someone who may be the soul mate, for example.)

And yet, Yoshimi hadn't experienced any, which made me suspect there might have been a fundamental problem with the way she was writing the wish. So I asked her how she usually wrote her wish. This was her response:

YOSHIMI: "How? I just write it straight: 'May I meet my soul mate as soon as possible.'"

KEIKO: "But you said you've been writing it for over a year?"

YOSHIMI: "That's right. Wait, it may be even longer. About a year and a half."

KEIKO: "So then you'd write it differently every once in a while, right?"

YOSHIMI: "No."

KEIKO: "What? So you write the exact same thing every time?"

YOSHIMI: "Yeah."

KEIKO: ". . ."

Sure, I understand you'd want to meet your soul mate as soon as possible. But I don't know about writing the same old thing over and over. Imagine a salesman trying to sell you the same thing ten or twenty times. Wouldn't you be sick of him? You wouldn't even want to listen to him, right? But what if he offered something else? If it's something different, you'd probably be willing to take a look. It may even be the thing you actually want.

The same goes for the Universe. Even if it hasn't listened

to a certain wish, there are plenty of chances for it to grant the wish if you write it differently. You need to vary the way you write your wishes.

You may want very much to meet your soul mate, but if all you write is "May I meet my soul mate as soon as possible," even the Universe will get tired of you. It has every right to think, "*This* again?"

I gave Yoshimi two pieces of advice. First, she should express sincere gratitude on the Full Moon in addition to wishing on the New Moon. And second, she should change the phrasing of her wish based on the current sign's area of expertise. For example, Leo is great at parties, so when the Moon is in Leo, she could add details like "at a barbecue" or "at a wedding reception." In the following month, Virgo governs workplaces, so she could include work-related details such as "when I visit client A's office" or "in my new project team."

When I explained this to Yoshimi, she nodded and said, "I see. I think I'm starting to get it." Starting with the following Full Moon, she began to tackle Power Wishes seriously. About a year later, during New Year's, she went to visit a friend in the United States. The friend hosted a party, where, lo and behold, Yoshimi met her soul mate! They got married shortly thereafter and now live together in Washington state.

Yoshimi told me that six months before the encounter, when the Full Moon was in Sagittarius, she wrote:

"My soul mate and I have decided to get married in a church in San Francisco with an ocean view! We're going to go pick out my wedding dress now. I never thought I could be so happy! Thank you so much!"

Sagittarius's area of expertise is overseas and foreign countries. To top it off, a church is one of the locations it governs. This is a prime example of how making a wish according to the sign of the Moon produces clear results.

Visualization speeds up manifestation

There are an infinite number of ways your wish could come true. Take a soul mate encounter, for example. You could meet them while traveling, as Yoshimi did, or you could meet them while in the hospital. I know of one case in which a job interviewer turned out to be a soul mate.

When it comes to the how, we just have to leave the Universe in charge. But there are things we can do. One of them is to visualize all kinds of possibilities and situations in which your wish could manifest.

Let your imagination wander according to the sign of the New Moon or Full Moon: *Wouldn't it be wonderful if it came true this way? It would be so cool if it came true that way! There's also the possibility of it coming true this way . . .* and so on. Once you hone your visualization skills like this and allow your subconscious to tie all the imagined scenes to your wish, nothing can stop you! Every action you take from here on out sets the stage upon which your wish will come true. Developing the subconscious in this way helps you become a strong and beautiful manifestation magnet.

If you don't feel confident in your visualization skills, you can use a Moon Collage (see page 255).

Power Wish Rule 3

Use Anchoring Statements and Anchorings.

Turn on the Universe's Wi-Fi with Anchoring Statements

Anchoring Statements are the very essence of the Keiko-Style Power Wish Method. It's important that you understand this.

One of the reasons why a wish you wrote may not come true is that you're not connected to the Universe. Making a wish without being connected to the Universe is like talking to yourself. It's as if you are on the phone chatting away when no one is on the other end. In other words, it's not a two-way conversation. Doesn't this seem pointless? To avoid this pitfall, make sure you use Anchoring Statements when you make a Power Wish.

Anchoring Statements are the magic words that plug you into the Universe. When you write these statements, you and the Universe can become well connected. You can think of it as turning on the Universe's Wi-Fi.

There are two types of Anchoring Statements: one for the New Moon and one for the Full Moon.

NEW MOON ANCHORING STATEMENTS

Write at the beginning of your New Moon Power Wish.

I am certain that the wish I am making is perfectly aligned with the will of the Universe, and that it is the highest and best way to bring love and prosperity into the world. Through the wish I am making, I intend for my love and power to quickly reach all beings everywhere.

FULL MOON ANCHORING STATEMENTS

Write at the beginning of your Full Moon Power Wish.

I am grateful that my wish has been granted in the fastest way possible by the guidance of the Universe. I pledge to share this happiness with the world in every way that I can. I am grateful that the love and the light of the Universe are always with me.

These are the opening statements I'd like you to write at the beginning of every Power Wish. They are not unlike a greeting in a letter, although while greetings may be mere formalities, Anchoring Statements have a clear purpose: to turn on the Universe's Wi-Fi and plug you into the Universe.

Anchoring Statements themselves already carry the highest vibration. You can copy and use them just as they are. If you speak them aloud as you write them down, that's even better. Writing alone is powerful enough, but if you turn these statements into the vibration of sound, they are transmitted to the Universe even faster.

Use Anchorings to make a presentation to the Universe

If Anchoring Statements are the opening of a Power Wish, Anchorings are the closing. By opening and closing with words that vibrate with the Universe, you unmistakably make your wish a Power Wish.

As with Anchoring Statements, there are different Anchorings for the New Moon and the Full Moon. Let me explain each separately.

New Moon Anchorings: "I intend to"
or "I intend for"

A New Moon is a state in which the Moon (feelings, emotions) and the Sun (will, intention) are perfectly aligned. This tells us that a New Moon is a time to align your feelings with your intentions—in other words, to make a resolution.

By putting your resolve into words and turning it into a vibration, you enable the Universe to receive it and create a reality to match. This is the mechanism of manifestation.

Phrases like "May I" and "I wish" are not effective for communicating your resolution. They don't convey resolve or declaration, do they? I wouldn't use the past tense here, either. Remember, the cycle of the Universe is that you sow seeds on a New Moon and reap them on a Full Moon, so only on a Full Moon does it makes sense to use the past tense. If you use the past tense on a New Moon, the Universe will just say, "Ah, I see that it's already come true for you," and your wish will be ignored.

A New Moon Power Wish is a declaration to the Universe. You'll be missing the point if you don't use phrases that convey your resolve.

Among the phrases that show resolve, "I intend to" is the most powerful. In my experience, I've found that when I write "I intend to," the wish manifests quickly and efficiently. Let me give you some examples to help you see this clearly.

NEW MOON POWER WISH EXAMPLES

"<u>I intend to</u> build a strong relationship of trust with Takehito and to support him as we share our lives together."

"<u>I intend to</u> meet my ideal partner who makes me a better person and to start a happy, cheerful family with him."

"<u>I intend to</u> lose five pounds for the audition in September."

"I intend to make my own needs my top priority and live the life I want, starting today."

"I intend to quit my job and go freelance before the end of the year."

All of these are Power Wishes previously written by me or my friends. Every single one of them has come true.

"I intend to" and "I intend for" are some of the Universe's favorite phrases. If you want to win the Universe's favor, you absolutely can't do without them! They are the most powerful Anchorings for the New Moon.

A New Moon wish is a presentation to the Universe. And with a New Moon Power Wish, you are making a stellar presentation that will win the Universe's favor.

A New Moon is the ideal opportunity for everyone to manifest their wishes. That being said, if you want reliable results, you need to put in the effort.

If all you do is make a laundry list of what you hope will happen, the Universe won't take notice. You've got to stand out. You've got to write your wish in such a way that it really shines and grabs the Universe's heart! If you do so, hopefully the Universe will think, "Wow, she is really motivated," or "It would be beneficial to manifest his wish." And when it does, congratulations—you're sure to be on its list of favorites! That's right, a Power Wish is the greatest tool to get you on the Universe's list of favorites.

> **Full Moon Anchorings:** A happy emotion or
> situation + "Thank you so much"

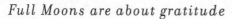

Full Moons are about gratitude

A Full Moon is a time to be grateful. It symbolizes harvest and completion. So asking the Universe to fulfill a wish during a Full Moon is like planting seeds in the winter—it goes against the flow of the Universe.

That being said, it's not that you can't write your wish on a Full Moon. You just have to write it in such a way that is appropriate for it.

A Full Moon is literally a Moon that is *full*. Its energy is a sense of fulfillment, such as "Thank you for a rich harvest" or "I'm so happy my wish came true." All you have to do is write your wish accordingly. You can still wish for the same thing as you did on the New Moon; just write it differently—make it the Full Moon version. That way, you can still write as many wishes as you like.

Take the New Moon Power Wishes on page 41, for example. If you were to rewrite them for the Full Moon, they would be like this:

FULL MOON POWER WISH EXAMPLES

Version 1: Giving thanks for what you'd like to manifest

"I am building a strong relationship of trust with Takehito and supporting him as we share our lives together. I am truly happy now. Thank you so much."

"I was able to meet my ideal partner who makes me a better person and have a happy, cheerful family

---

with him. Every day is filled with so much love, <u>it's like a dream. Thank you so much</u>."

"I succeeded in losing five pounds for the audition in September. <u>I couldn't feel more confident! Thank you so much</u>."

"I am now living the life I want with my own needs as my top priority. As a result, <u>I feel so motivated and fulfilled every day! Thank you so much</u>."

"I quit my job and started freelancing. Projects are flooding in one after another. <u>I'm so happy I could scream! Thank you so much</u>."

Do you see how they are wishing for the same thing, but they've written it differently? The basic principle of a Full Moon Power Wish is to write it as if it has already come true (you can use past or present tense). Whether it actually came true or not, it's important that you thank the Universe under the assumption that it has already granted your wish.

Another important thing to include is at least one happy

emotion or positive phrase, like "I feel blessed," "It's like a dream," or even expressions like "I'm so happy!" "Awesome!" or "Yay!" There are no set rules on this, so go ahead and write what you'd like to feel or experience when the wish comes true.

If you can't think of the right words, you can write, "Everything is going my way!"

Imagining in advance what it would feel like when the wish comes true is one of the most effective techniques to use with a Full Moon Power Wish.

Pretending the wish already came true makes it come true

As far as Full Moon Power Wishes are concerned, it's not important whether they have actually come true. The key is to visualize the wish coming true, really feel how happy it makes you, and offer gratitude to the Universe in advance.

The truth of the matter is, wishes often come true when you feel like they already have. There may be a bit of a time lag, but that's insignificant. "It's going to come true sooner or later, so why don't I thank the Universe in advance?" is the kind of attitude that's most likely going to manifest the wish. Everyone in my circle of friends who is manifesting one wish after another, including me, has this attitude of "Oh well, it's going to come true sooner or later."

At any rate, there's no such thing as giving too much thanks. Even without the wishing part, if you make a habit of expressing gratitude on the Full Moon, that alone will surely increase your luck and bring you plenty of happiness.

Our tendency is to focus on lack. *I don't have this, I don't have that, other people have it and I don't*, and so on. We focus so much on what we don't have that we often don't notice that in fact we've already been given so much.

The key to manifesting is not to ask for what you don't have, but to be grateful for what you do have. Appreciate the happiness that's yours right now, and say thank you to your parents, ancestors, and everyone around you who has contributed to that happiness. And last but not least, don't forget to thank the Universe.

Be grateful for synchronicity and serendipity

When writing a Full Moon Power Wish, it's also great to write about something that happened recently that made you happy. For example:

FULL MOON POWER WISH EXAMPLES

Version 2: Giving thanks for happy moments

"I was gifted with a ticket to see a play that I really wanted to see. <u>What luck! I'm super lucky! Thank you so much!</u>"

"Just when I had a craving for cream puffs, Mr. Yamazaki brought us a whole box. <u>It was totally the law of attraction! Thank you so much, Mr. Yamazaki!</u>"

"Just when I needed to catch a cab, one stopped right in front of me to drop someone off. <u>It's a miracle that I didn't have to wait at all for a cab when it was raining! Thank you so much!</u>"

"I stopped by the flower shop during my lunch break, and there were so many Casablanca lilies—my favorite! <u>I enjoyed a moment of bliss as I was surrounded by the sweet smell. Thank you so much.</u>"

Just like this, I recommend you write out not only the small synchronicities, but also every instance in which you thought, "I'm so lucky!" "Oh my god, I'm so happy!" "Wow, I'm pretty amazing," and so on. As far as these are concerned, you don't have to worry about the themes of the twelve zodiac signs. Whatever it is, the important thing is to remember that it happened and it made you happy. By doing so, you will naturally be aligned with the Full Moon energy. And don't forget the closing phrase: "Thank you so much."

The vibration of gratitude is the same as that of love. The more you give thanks, the more love you'll have within you. Once you are completely filled with love, you will begin to emit an extremely high vibration, and eventually you'll be on the same wavelength as the Universe, which also has a high vibration. Only then can you become a presence that the Universe recognizes.

Once the Universe acknowledges you as a being of high vibration, your good fortune is pretty much guaranteed. Almost any kind of wish you make will be granted. After all, your name has made the Universe's favorites list.

*The Full Moon is also a time to write down
anything you want to let go of*

There is another thing you can write on a Full Moon that can produce amazing results: anything you want to release. In other words, during a Full Moon, you can make not only Power Wishes but also Release Wishes.

When the Moon gradually wanes after a Full Moon, it's literally releasing—or letting go of—the energy that made it full. This energy of releasing is super useful.

We are great at hoarding, but when it comes to letting go, not so much. If we let our guard down, we can easily gain weight or extra fat. Have you noticed how so many people are still holding on to past traumas, broken hearts, jealousy, or anger? Or perhaps you have an unhealthy habit that you can't quit, no matter how hard you've tried?

Whether they are emotions or habits, it's difficult to let go of things once they have become a part of us. I think it's pretty challenging to let go of these through willpower alone. But when we have the support and power of a Full Moon, it's not that difficult anymore; we can let them go quite naturally.

All you have to do is ride the wave of "release mode"

You see, during a Full Moon, the entire Universe is in "release mode," so for us, it's as easy as riding that wave. We can become a suckerfish to the Universe's shark. All we have to do is to let the flow take over.

That said, this should also be done according to the zodiac sign that the Full Moon is in. As I've explained, each of the twelve signs has a specific area of expertise. As a matter of fact, each of them is also tied to certain emotions and qualities. For example, Aries is related to anger, frustration, and impatience; Taurus, to stubbornness, attachment, and slowness; Virgo, to fussiness, anxiety, and criticism; and so on.

So if you are struggling to let go of your attachment to someone, then write something like this when the Full Moon is in Taurus: "My attachment to Alex is naturally gone." If you don't want to fret over small things anymore, then write something like this when the Full Moon is in Virgo: "I'm no longer fretting over small things."

A Full Moon is a time for gratitude as well as release. As

for specific lists of what can be released, please see the appropriate zodiac sign–specific pages in part two.

Power Wish Rule 4

Incorporate Power Words (words that easily connect to the Universe).

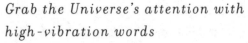

Grab the Universe's attention with high-vibration words

The secret to Power Wishing is to use Anchoring Statements and Anchorings. The reason why these are necessary is that they are powerful and have a high vibration, which means they instantly connect you to the Universe.

High-vibration words are like a loud bell ringing. The higher the vibration of the words you use, the louder the bell rings, and the faster you can connect to the Universe. The Universe notices you right away.

On the contrary, no matter how enthusiastically you

write, if you are using low-vibration words, the Universe won't notice, because the ringing is too quiet. Think of high-vibration words as tools to help you get the Universe's attention.

Interestingly, low-vibration people can't use high-vibration words. It's not that they *don't* use them; they can't. For example, they hardly ever write or speak the word *love*. They also feel uncomfortable with high-vibration words like *gratitude* and *trust*. By "low-vibration people," I mean those who are living in anger, hatred, jealousy, attachment, grievances, and other negative thoughts, emotions, and behavioral patterns. As the Universal law of attraction dictates, things that share the same vibration are drawn to one another, so low-vibration people are more familiar with low-vibration words—they feel comfortable with them. In other words, your own vibration is always linked to the vibration of the words you can use.

That said, it's also perfectly possible to take advantage of this principle. Just as people who are unhealthy can improve their health by, for example, eating quality meals, you can raise your vibration by using high-vibration words. This is what's fascinating about vibrations.

In fact, just by using Anchoring Statements and Anchorings

every New Moon and Full Moon, your vibration naturally rises. Your Power Wishes become more likely to come true each time you write them, because your own vibration rises each time, which makes you increasingly appealing to the Universe.

Anchoring Statements in particular are not only incredibly high in vibration, but they are also the magic words to plug you in to the Universe. Saying them out loud like a magic spell every day will raise your vibration and increase the chances of your wishes coming true.

Power Wishing is the process of aligning your vibration with the Universe

The world is made up of vibrations. Thoughts, consciousness, and emotions are all vibrations. And each one of them has its own vibration, attracting things from the same dimension.

TV and radio work the same way. If you turn the TV to the sports channel, you'll be watching sports. Similarly, if you were to switch your consciousness channel to "gratitude," it would lead you to information, people, and situations of a corresponding vibration. If you switch the channel to "anger," it will lead you to things corresponding to that vibration. As the law of the Universe dictates, like attracts like. Things of the same vibration are drawn to one another.

The Keiko-Style Power Wish Method applies this principle to writing. By incorporating high-vibration words such as expressions of gratitude and love, the Power Wish Method turns the task of writing a wish into a powerful action that aligns your vibration with the Universe. (See pages 60–61 for examples of high-vibration Power Words.)

Since words have clear vibrations, the more high-vibration words you use, the bigger and stronger your pipeline to the Universe becomes. Furthermore, if you say them aloud as you write them, you can amplify this effect even more.

Sound is air vibrating. Along with visualization, it's one of the best ways to connect to the Universe. High-vibration words have especially high frequencies and can easily reach the Universe. When you say high-vibration words aloud as you write them, your own vibration grows higher and higher, until you and the Universe are literally on the same wavelength.

By the way, Power Wishes should be written by hand, as

a basic principle. If you use a computer, the electromagnetic wave blocks the vibration of the Moon.

Power Wish Rule 5

Finish writing within ten hours of the
New Moon or the Full Moon.

Making a Power Wish is essentially about planting the seeds of possibility.

I once met an expert rose gardener who told me, "If you want to grow a magnificent rose, it's crucial to plant the seed at the right time." The same goes for Power Wishes. If you want your wish to come true, you have to time it effectively.

The basic rule of the Power Wish Method is to finish writing your wish within ten hours of the accurate New Moon or Full Moon time. If that's not possible, you can write it within twenty-four hours.

This ten-hour recommendation is based on my years of experimenting with Power Wishes. This is the time frame I found to be the most effective. Understand that the effect will diminish when you write it outside this ten-hour window. That said, the Power Wish doesn't lose all of its effect, so if you still have time to write yours within a twenty-four-hour window, it's worth it.

On the other hand, I'd like you to be careful not to make a false start. The Universe's vibration becomes a bit unstable just before a New Moon or Full Moon. The purpose of a Power Wish is to firmly anchor your wish to the Universe. You want the conditions to be as stable as possible before you lower the anchor, so I recommend writing it *after* the exact New Moon or Full Moon time.

Example 1

DECEMBER 14, 2020: NEW MOON IN SAGITTARIUS
The precise New Moon time is 11:16 A.M. EST. (Go to keiko powerwish.com to look up the precise time of the New Moon.) Finish writing the Power Wish before 9:16 P.M. EST the same day (if that's not possible, then before 11:16 A.M. EST on December 15).

Example 2

DECEMBER 29, 2020: FULL MOON IN CANCER

The precise Full Moon time is 10:28 P.M. EST. Finish writing the Power Wish before 8:28 A.M. EST on December 30 (if that's not possible, then before 10:28 P.M. EST on December 30).

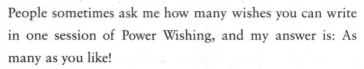

Power Wish Rule 6

You can make as many wishes as you like!

People sometimes ask me how many wishes you can write in one session of Power Wishing, and my answer is: As many as you like!

The Universe is incredibly open and super generous. It never says petty things like "You're only allowed ten wishes at a time" or "I don't grant wishes to greedy people." You can also be assured that the number of your wishes has no effect on how fast they come true, either. So whether it's five or ten or a hundred, go ahead and write as many wishes as you like.

POWER WISH RULES REVIEW

1. Write your wishes as intentions on the New Moon; write them as statements of gratitude on the Full Moon.
2. Note the area of expertise for each zodiac sign that the New Moon or the Full Moon is in.
3. Use Anchoring Statements and Anchorings.
4. Incorporate Power Words (words that easily connect to the Universe; see pages 60–61 for a list of Power Words).
5. Finish writing within ten hours of the New Moon or Full Moon; if that's impossible, finish within twenty-four hours.
6. You can make as many wishes as you like, or just one focused wish.

LIST OF POWER WORDS

⚷ **special phrases:** Thank you; I am grateful; Thanks to . . .

⚷ love, hope, gratitude, happiness, bliss, passion, awe, joy, health, prayer, trust, courage, good, light, dream, ideal, harmony, peace, prosperity, success, glory, abundance, relief, fulfillment, miracle, power

⚷ happy, glad, fun, exciting, cheerful, beautiful, wonderful, kind, lucky, like a dream, bright, delightful, pure, perfect, blissful, supreme, premium, radiant, stunning, sparkling, brilliant, comfortable, pleasant, fulfilled, overflowing, uplifting, magnificent, splendid, unbelievable

⚷ abundantly, comfortably, freely, newly, with everyone, for everyone, for the society, for the world, confidently, sincerely, faithfully, earnestly, genuinely, bravely, pleasantly, with a smile, refreshingly, smoothly, easily, with ease, just like that, without difficulty, without struggle, efficiently, fluently, fluidly, melodiously, effortlessly, willingly, soundly, healthily, steadily, quickly, rapidly, all at once, casually, naturally, in a natural way, without a hitch, before I knew it

be moved, forgive, love, believe, trust, polish, purify, give, reward, share, accept, watch over, nurture, raise, grow, expand, unfold, make progress, take delight in, enjoy, release, revel in, be fulfilled, be full of, be relieved, be all right, be stable, praise, compliment, applaud

Note: It's better not to use forceful words or phrases, such as "absolutely," "at any cost," "no matter what," "must," or "insist," because they don't resonate with the Universe.

How to Write a Power Wish for Others

Many of my readers ask me questions such as "If I'm wishing for my husband's success instead of for my own, should

I write my wish the same way?" or "My mother is ill. How do I write a Power Wish for her recovery?"

For example, let's take this question from Hinako:

> "With Power Wish, can we make wishes for someone else? For example, I want my son to pass the high school entrance exam . . . I want my husband to get a raise . . . etc. And I also want my mother to recover from her illness. I'm sure there are many people who are wondering the same thing. Please let me know your thoughts!"

Of course it's possible to write a wish for someone else using the Power Wish Method. However, I doubt your wish will come true if you write it like this:

"I intend for my son to get accepted into high school."

"I intend for my husband to get a raise."

"I intend for my mother to feel better again."

When you write a Power Wish about someone else, make sure to include what you can do for that person. For example, if Hinako were to make her wishes on the Leo New Moon, she could write them like this:

> I intend to create the perfect environment for my son Tatsuya to study effectively for his entrance exam, and to provide him with mental and emotional support.
>
> I intend to offer maximum support to my husband so that his hard work will be rightly rewarded and result in his promotion and a raise.
>
> I intend to share a meal with my mother at least once a week and have uplifting conversations that can help her smile again.

How's that? Do you get the point? "I want my son to study hard for his entrance exam. I want him to get into his first choice school."—all parents would think that. So then what can *you* do for him? How can *you* support him? That's the important part.

A Power Wish is something you manifest through yourself, whether you're wishing for yourself or for others. If you want to wish someone happiness or change their circumstances, you first have to change how you interact with that person. That's the surest and fastest way.

Therefore, instead of "I intend for Alex to fall in love with me," try:

I intend to become a gorgeous woman who captivates Alex.

I intend to become an attractive woman whom Alex loves dearly.

You see? Again, don't forget, whether you're wishing for yourself or others, you are the only one who can manifest the wish.

PART 2

Harness the 12 Zodiac Signs' Areas of Expertise

New Moon and Full Moon
Power Wish Examples and
Guidelines for Every Sign

FOR ALL SIGNS

NEW MOON ANCHORING STATEMENTS

Anchoring Statements are the magic words that plug you into the Universe. Write them at the beginning of your New Moon Power Wish.

I am certain that the wish I am making is perfectly aligned with the will of the Universe, and that it is the highest and best way to bring love and prosperity into the world. Through the wish I am making, I intend for my love and power to quickly reach all beings everywhere.

NEW MOON ANCHORINGS

Anchorings are the magic words that deliver your wishes to the Universe. Use them to close your New Moon Power Wish.

I intend to . . . / I intend for . . .

FOR ALL SIGNS

FULL MOON ANCHORING STATEMENTS

Anchoring Statements are the magic words that plug you into the Universe. Write them at the beginning of your Full Moon Power Wish.

I am grateful that my wish has been granted in the fastest way possible by the guidance of the Universe. I pledge to share this happiness with the world in every way that I can. I am grateful that the love and the light of the Universe are always with me.

FULL MOON ANCHORINGS

Anchorings are the magic words that deliver your wishes to the Universe. Use them to close your Full Moon Power Wish.

A happy emotion or situation + Thank you so much

1

New Moon and Full Moon In

ARIES

CHALLENGE YOURSELF
AND CLAIM VICTORY

Aries Power Wishes

Carve out a new path with the New Moon.

Banish fear and reluctance with the Full Moon.

When you want to drive somewhere, you first start the car, right? You insert a key or press a button, turn on the engine, shift into gear, and step on the gas pedal. This is essentially the energy of Aries.

Just start moving, without a second thought. Create a flow. Aries's role is to build something from the ground up and see that it takes off.

When you want to launch a business, start a new job, build a relationship with someone, or get a fresh start in a new field, be sure to take advantage of Aries Power Wishes. An Aries New Moon or Full Moon is also helpful when you are at the end of a cycle and want to move on to a new stage.

As you know, Aries is the first of the twelve signs of the zodiac—the leadoff hitter. Since the purpose of the leadoff hitter is to get on base, the propelling force of Aries is second to none. And it's also fast! Any wish you make on a New Moon or Full Moon in Aries unfolds more quickly than with any other sign. When you want a project or idea to come to life as soon as possible, the New Moon and Full Moon in Aries will lend you great power.

Aries provides you with all the elements you need to succeed, whether it's the courage to bring your thoughts into action without second-guessing yourself, decisiveness, or a can-do attitude. And above all else, it gifts you with a rock-solid conviction that you can carve out your life with your own hands, instead of waiting for it to happen.

If you have something you want to try but haven't been able to put it into action, write specifically about what you want to start doing. Aries Power Wishes can also be intensely effective when you're feeling down and want to light a fire under yourself.

Aries New Moon Power Wish

Late March to Late April

An Aries New Moon helps you . . .

+ Start something new
+ Make situations unfold more quickly
+ Leave a company in order to start your own business or to become independent
+ Tackle a challenge with courage
+ Come out on top
+ Go forth in your chosen path
+ Overcome setbacks to claim victory
+ Live an authentic life
+ Make it a habit to live by intuition

◈

- ✦ With anything related to sports and exercise
- ✦ With anything related to the face, hair, or head

Inquiries from the Universe

To help you find clues when you don't know what to write

- ✦ What would you like to start doing?
- ✦ What would you like to unfold more quickly?
- ✦ What is something you'd really like to overcome?
- ✦ What would you like to be number one at?
- ✦ What is something you'd really like to ace?

TOP 3 POWER WISH EXAMPLES THAT ARE LIKELY TO COME TRUE WITH AN ARIES NEW MOON

1. <u>I intend for</u> my new life to begin brightly this very day.
2. <u>I intend to</u> embrace every opportunity and be brave enough to challenge myself.
3. <u>I intend to</u> carve out my own chosen path without being swayed by others.

RECOMMENDED KEYWORDS FOR ARIES POWER WISHES

Start

beginning, departure, energy, agility, off to a good start, fast, progress, expand, initiative

⚷ *Courage*

enthusiasm, passion, fight, intuition, calmness under pressure, competitiveness, independence, strong will, motivation, vitality, spirit

⚷ *Uniqueness*

authenticity, original, only one, pioneer, first, discover, the world's first, America's first, first in history

⚷ *Independence*

start a business, go out on my own, open a business, open a store, open up, trailblaze

⚷ *Be proactive*

take the first step, discover, carve out, go forward, move ahead, have courage, take a chance, triumph, overcome, come out on top, become number one, make up my mind, train, exercise

⚊⊕ *Challenge*

passionately, boldly, quickly, powerfully, actively, bravely, strongly, enthusiastically, fearlessly, optimistically, dynamically, suddenly, in the blink of an eye, increasingly, more and more

⚊⊕ *Exercise*

gym, fitness, sports, muscular strength

ROMANTIC RELATIONSHIPS AND PARTNERSHIPS

✦ I intend to meet my perfect match and to start a completely new life from a clean slate.

✦ I intend to end my current relationship amicably and meet my soul mate at the perfect time.

CAREER AND BUSINESS

✦ I intend for my business project to unfold quickly and dynamically.

✦ I intend to open up a salon in a prime location as soon as I possibly can.

✦ I intend to transfer to the marketing department and start a new career within one year.

FINANCES

✦ I intend to find a new source of income and to double my income.

✦ I intend to find my dream job and become financially independent within six months.

✦ I intend to make a comfortable living doing work that I can be truly proud of.

HABITS

✦ I intend to wake up at six and practice half an hour of yoga every morning.

✦ From this point on, I intend to value my own feelings more than the opinions of others.

PERSONALITY

✦ I intend to become a new, proactive version of myself, turning intuition immediately into initiative.

✦ I intend to become a brave new version of myself, constantly tackling new challenges.

HEALTH AND BEAUTY

✦ I intend to begin doing personal training sessions twice a week this April, building muscle and mental strength so I can pursue my goals decisively.

✦ I intend to get a new haircut as I launch my own business, making a fresh, bold start in my new, challenging career.

MISCELLANEOUS

✦ I intend to move out of my childhood home and start living in my own place within a year.

✦ I intend to move to a new town and give myself a fresh new start as soon as possible.

Aries Full Moon Power Wish

Late September to Late October

The themes and keywords are the same as those for the New Moon. Additionally, an Aries Full Moon helps you release . . .

- Impatience, hastiness, impulsiveness, or hot-temperedness
- Anger; frustration; jealousy toward a competitor
- Troubles or worries about the head, face, or hair; headaches

TOP 2 POWER/RELEASE WISH
EXAMPLES THAT ARE LIKELY
TO COME TRUE WITH AN ARIES
FULL MOON

1. The new store I opened has been getting great reviews, and thankfully the sales are increasing every month, too. <u>Everything is as I envisioned! Thank you so much.</u>
2. I've now made it a habit to take action as soon as I have an intuition. Life has picked up its pace, and <u>I'm totally in the flow! Thank you so much.</u>

ROMANTIC RELATIONSHIPS AND PARTNERSHIPS

✦ I met a beautiful woman at my gym, and we started going out. I'm blown away by how fast things are moving. Thank you so much.

CAREER AND BUSINESS

✦ I kept my motivation up and became the top seller in the sales department! I've never felt so good! Thank you so much.

FINANCES

✦ Ever since I was featured in a lifestyle magazine, I've been getting more great clients and my sales numbers have gone through the roof. It excites me to think about what's coming next! Thank you so much.

HABITS

✦ I'm getting used to taking the stairs in the subway. I love how much more fit I feel. Thank you so much!

PERSONALITY

✦ I'm no longer the coward who used to give up without trying. I enjoy challenging myself now! Thank you so much.

HEALTH AND BEAUTY

✦ Since I started doing mindfulness exercises in the morning, I've been getting fewer and fewer migraines, and now they've disappeared completely! I feel so blessed to be able to go through each day with comfort and ease. Thank you so much!

MISCELLANEOUS

✦ My longtime dream of watching the Grand Sumo Tournament live has come true! I was blown away by the intensity of the matches and found the traditional Japanese aesthetics and rituals fascinating. It was such an exciting day! Thank you so much.

2

New Moon and Full Moon In

TAURUS

GAIN FINANCIAL
STABILITY AND
ABUNDANCE

Taurus Power Wishes

Create an abundant flow of money with the
New Moon.

Release the "poor" mind-set with the Full Moon.

Once Aries gets things off to a good start, Taurus's job is to create wealth and abundance. Taurus is one of the signs that rule money and material possessions.

Money is a necessity. And yet, so many people don't have enough of it and are struggling. If you are one of them, I highly recommend you make Taurus Power Wishes.

Taurus Power Wishes are very effective. This is because the Taurus New Moon is immediately preceded or followed by the Scorpio Full Moon, and the Taurus Full Moon is immediately preceded or followed by the Scorpio New Moon.

Of all the zodiac signs, Taurus and Scorpio are the two big ones for finances. Both of them strongly attract money or possessions and have the power to anchor and stabilize that flow once it's created.

The original meaning of Taurus is the innate talent and character each person is born with. We all have unique aptitudes and dispositions, and when we use them to serve others and help the world, money is what we receive.

The first step is to express your core skills and qualities. Then, if you write a Taurus Power Wish on top of that, the Universe is sure to create the flow that will turn these gifts into money.

Aside from finances, Taurus rules anything that you'd like to stabilize or sustain. A wavering relationship can be transformed into a solid one with the help of a Taurus Power Wish.

Taurus New Moon Power Wish

Late April to Late May

A Taurus New Moon helps you . . .

- ✦ Live a prosperous and comfortable life
- ✦ Stabilize what you have already begun
- ✦ Make certain what is uncertain
- ✦ Improve your quality of life
- ✦ Increase income and wealth
- ✦ Be fulfilled financially and materially
- ✦ Turn your talent and character into income
- ✦ Focus on one thing with patience
- ✦ Nurture a solid and steady romantic relationship
- ✦ Relish all the abundance that life has to offer

✦ With anything related to the neck, throat, voice, or thyroid

Inquiries from the Universe

To help you find clues when you don't know what to write

✦ What would you like to bring stability to?
✦ How much income would you like?
✦ What would give you a sense of safety?
✦ What do you need in order to feel like you have more than enough?
✦ When do you feel fulfilled?

TOP 3 POWER WISH EXAMPLES THAT ARE LIKELY TO COME TRUE WITH A TAURUS NEW MOON

1. <u>I intend for</u> twenty thousand dollars to consistently flow into my bank account every month.
2. <u>I intend to</u> earn more than enough money to fully enjoy all the pleasures of life.
3. <u>I intend to</u> have the money to build the house I want by the end of this year.

RECOMMENDED KEYWORDS FOR TAURUS POWER WISHES

Money

income, wealth, asset, finance, financial stability, comfortable life, can afford, lifestyle, value

⚷ *Talent*

aesthetic sense, the five senses, sensibility, art, expertise, craftsmanship, innate, inherent

⚷ *Nature*

plants, flowers, trees, green, earth, organic, natural, ecology, texture, grounding

⚷ *Abundant*

comfortable, pleasant, rich, ample, sufficient, lavish, luxurious, high-class, superior, high-quality, valuable, real

⚷ *Reliably*

steadily, consistently, one step at a time, safely, adequately, in a relaxed manner, every week, every month, on a regular basis, right here and now, generously, faithfully

---

⚿ *Stabilize*

be fulfilled, make certain, continue, sustain, accumulate, feel safe, be blessed, enjoy, fully relish

---

ROMANTIC RELATIONSHIPS AND PARTNERSHIPS

+ I intend to marry someone who shares my values and for us to be faithful to each other for the rest of our lives.

+ I intend to meet someone and for us to live a happy and comfortable life together.

CAREER AND BUSINESS

+ I intend to get a job within the next six months that allows me to fully express my aesthetic sense.

+ I intend to become an independent financial planner and succeed as an expert in my field.

FINANCES

✦ I intend for enough money to consistently flow into my bank account every month so that I can enjoy a luxurious lifestyle.

✦ I intend to earn enough money to allow me to go to the spa or the beauty salon every week.

HABITS

✦ From this moment on, I intend to spend time only on things I find truly valuable.

✦ I intend to garden on the weekends, recharging my energy by being in nature.

PERSONALITY

✦ I intend to commit to following through on what I start, instead of giving up halfway

✦ I intend to take steady steps toward my dream without comparing myself to others.

HEALTH AND BEAUTY

- ✦ I intend to eat only what's good for my body, starting today.
- ✦ I intend to commit to a daily routine of five minutes of stretching before bedtime.

MISCELLANEOUS

- ✦ I intend to easily raise the money I need to open an organic café.
- ✦ I intend to meet a new partner and get engaged before my next birthday.

Taurus Full Moon Power Wish

Late October to Late November

The themes and keywords are the same as those for the New Moon. Additionally, a Taurus Full Moon helps you release . . .

+ Stubbornness, inflexibility
+ Attachment, fear of loss, being a sore loser
+ Troubles or worries about the throat, neck, voice, or thyroid

TOP 2 POWER/RELEASE WISH
EXAMPLES THAT ARE LIKELY
TO COME TRUE WITH A TAURUS
FULL MOON

1. I have no more difficulty with or anxiety about money. I am relishing the feeling of limitless abundance showering upon me right now. Thank you so much.
2. My attachment to money and material things has naturally disappeared. I now have the confidence to effortlessly attract what I need! Thank you so much.

ROMANTIC RELATIONSHIPS AND PARTNERSHIPS

✦ My relationship with Noah has become increasingly stable, and we are finding ourselves naturally talking about our future together. I am so grateful for this huge progress! Thank you so much.

CAREER AND BUSINESS

✦ I'm opening my own boutique of hand-picked products that reflect my sensibility. And it's in my dream location! Thank you so much.

FINANCES

✦ My monthly income is now over fifteen thousand dollars, which allows me to buy things without worrying about the price. I am very happy! Thank you so much.

HABITS

✦ I can now allow myself to indulge every once in a while without feeling guilty. This is all thanks to the abundant flow of money I'm receiving. Thank you so much.

PERSONALITY

✦ I used to be so stubborn, but now I can't believe how flexible I've become. Now that I'm not bickering with my partner anymore, I feel very peaceful. Thank you so much.

HEALTH AND BEAUTY

✦ Thanks to the neck massages I've been giving myself, I can now see my neckline slimming down and my collarbone becoming beautifully pronounced. I'm going to look great in a halter dress this summer! Thank you so much.

MISCELLANEOUS

✦ Since learning the principle that money grows when I let it flow, I've been able to use money generously for others. What I give always comes back to me in multiples, and I am feeling more and more financially secure. Thank you so much.

3

New Moon and Full Moon In

GEMINI

SEIZE THE OPPORTUNITY
AT THE PERFECT TIME

♊

Gemini Power Wishes

Ride the wave of opportunity with the New Moon.

Say goodbye to a monotonous life with the
Full Moon.

G ood fortune is all about timing. No matter how talented
you are or how hard you work, if your timing isn't right,
you won't get results, and success becomes difficult. Whether
your wish comes true also depends on timing.

The zodiac sign that rules the timing of all things is
Gemini. If you think you always have terrible timing, you
should make good use of Gemini Power Wishes.

Good timing is all about receiving the right information
at the right time. If you have been searching for months and
still can't find the connection or the information you need,

it's highly likely that you lack the energy of Gemini. Use Gemini Power Wishes to attract the best information.

Lady Luck is terribly quick to run away. We need to be fast on our feet in order to nimbly ride one wave of opportunity after another. You don't need hard work to get luck on your side. Once you use Gemini Power Wishes to get yourself in the right place at the right time, luck will naturally find you.

Gemini, along with Aquarius (page 209), has become increasingly important in recent years. This is because Gemini rules information.

In our information age, we're constantly exchanging emails, in both our professional and personal lives. There are more people who own a smartphone than not. Gemini happens to be the sign that governs everything pertaining to information and transmission. Words and communication are also ruled by Gemini. It's not hard to see how significant a sign it is.

Gemini represents curiosity and variety. It's great at developing multiple things simultaneously, so if you have a long list of things you want to manifest, Gemini Power Wishes are sure to be of great help. If what you are longing for is a stimulating life full of changes, entrust it to a Gemini Power Wish.

Gemini New Moon Power Wish

Late May to Late June

A Gemini New Moon helps you . . .

- Communicate clearly and with precision
- Receive the perfect information at the perfect time
- Work and succeed in multiple fields simultaneously
- Enjoy unforced conversations no matter whom you are with
- Expand possibilities by studying what interests you
- Adapt to a new environment
- Live an active life with ease
- Profit from a second source of income
- Gain worldly wisdom

◈

+ With anything related to the hands, arms, lungs, and respiratory system

Inquiries from the Universe

To help you find clues when you don't know what to write

+ What would you like to learn right now?
+ What are you interested in but haven't pursued?
+ What is on your bucket list?
+ What can you teach others?
+ If you could obtain two things at once, what would they be?

TOP 3 POWER WISH EXAMPLES THAT ARE LIKELY TO COME TRUE WITH A GEMINI NEW MOON

1. <u>I intend to</u> communicate joyfully and skillfully with everyone and cultivate harmonious relationships.
2. <u>I intend to</u> always receive the exact information I need at the perfect time.
3. <u>I intend to</u> easily balance my work and personal lives, simultaneously enjoying happiness in both areas.

RECOMMENDED KEYWORDS FOR GEMINI POWER WISHES

Information

knowledge, learning, study, writing, words, composition, book, reading, communication, conversation, speech, smartphone, social media, blog, newsletter, trend, negotiation, wit, joke, humor, idea, thought, curiosity, input, output, second job, side business

⚷ *Move*

commute, transfer, travel, business trip, overnight stay, mini-vacation, bicycle, cycling

⚷ *Peers*

friend, childhood friend, classmate, colleague, sibling, neighbor, friendship, couple, pair, partner

⚷ *Intelligent*

well-rounded, versatile, multi-, friendly, eloquent, fascinating, cool, fresh, light, a variety of

⚷ *Flexibly*

both, either, simultaneously, at the same time, nimbly, lightly, rhythmically, easily, shallowly and widely, at the perfect time

---

⚯ *Communicate*

talk, explain, teach, write, learn, experience, adapt, adjust, grasp the situation, catch, befriend, post (to social media)

ROMANTIC RELATIONSHIPS AND PARTNERSHIPS

✦ I intend to meet the most fun partner, with whom I can talk for hours without ever feeling bored.

✦ I intend for my friendship with Sam to soon blossom into a romantic relationship.

CAREER AND BUSINESS

✦ I intend to hold workshops as a personal branding coach all over the United States, easily bringing in more than two hundred people every time.

✦ I intend to debut as a screenwriter before the end of the year and become highly sought-after as quickly as possible.

FINANCES

+ I intend to have a second job in the art world and bring in just as much income as my primary job.

+ I intend to bring in income in various ways without being attached to one particular job.

HABITS

+ I intend to travel every two months, broadening my horizons and experiences.

+ I intend to understand the importance of words, making a conscious effort to use only words that are beautiful and good.

PERSONALITY

+ I intend to take action enthusiastically, instead of suppressing my curiosity to see and learn.

+ I intend to live cheerfully and lightheartedly, never forgetting to have a sense of humor no matter what happens.

HEALTH AND BEAUTY

+ I intend to roll my shoulder blades twenty times every day, creating "angel wings" and slimming down my shoulders.

+ I intend to become healthier by drinking a glass of water with lemon juice every morning.

MISCELLANEOUS

+ I intend to choose a job that fulfills my intellectual curiosity, balancing my learning with my income.

+ I intend to ignore gossip and listen only to positive news.

Gemini Full Moon Power Wish

Late November to Late December

The themes and keywords are the same as those for the New Moon. Additionally, a Gemini Full Moon helps you release . . .

+ Lack of commitment, lack of focus, being easily bored
+ Being flaky or two-faced, internet addiction
+ Troubles or worries about the hands, arms, respiratory system; seasonal allergies

---

TOP 2 POWER/RELEASE WISH
EXAMPLES THAT ARE LIKELY TO
COME TRUE WITH A GEMINI
FULL MOON

1. <u>I am thankful</u> that the information I need always comes to me at the perfect time. <u>I am also grateful for the many synchronicities that have been happening! Thank you so much.</u>
2. I am no longer shy around strangers. Lately, <u>I'm having so much fun</u> meeting new people! <u>I am so excited</u> that my world is expanding. <u>Thank you so much.</u>

ROMANTIC RELATIONSHIPS AND PARTNERSHIPS

+ I had my first conversation with Dylan, whom I've admired for a long time. We are now friends, and I can't wait to see how our relationship unfolds. Thank you so much.

CAREER AND BUSINESS

✦ I got a stimulating job that keeps me on my toes. It's so nice to be able to enjoy my work. Thank you so much.

FINANCES

✦ My social media campaign was a success, and my revenue has doubled! I'm going to keep riding this wave all the way. Thank you so much.

HABITS

✦ I realize that I have been doing voice lessons for over a year now. I'm no longer the person who couldn't stick to anything! Thank you so much.

PERSONALITY

✦ I'm now getting in the habit of listening and letting others finish what they have to say before I speak. Thanks to this, I don't jump to conclusions nearly as much as I used to. Thank you so much.

HEALTH AND BEAUTY

✦ Since moving to a house by the beach, I've been miraculously relieved of seasonal allergies. I'm so glad I took a leap of faith and decided to move! Thank you so much.

MISCELLANEOUS

✦ I am deeply content that I can now go wherever I like, see whomever I like, and experience whatever I like. I feel so alive when I'm learning something new! Thank you so much.

4

New Moon and Full Moon In

CANCER

BUILD A HAPPY FAMILY
FULL OF LOVE

Cancer Power Wishes

Create a place of safety and belonging with
the New Moon.

Let go of unstable emotions with the Full Moon.

Many of you may be longing to marry the love of your life, be blessed with children, and build happy families. Cancer Power Wishes take charge of all of these for you.

Cancer is a sign that rules everything pertaining to family life: marriage with a beloved partner, pregnancy, childbirth, parenting, and even relationships with children, parents, and extended family.

Considering how households and family relationships are the very foundation of our lives, the potential role that Cancer Power Wishes could play in them is immeasurable.

No matter what happens, I have family and friends whom I love—Cancer provides you with that sense of safety and belonging.

If fortune is all about timing, then happiness is all about your household. If your household is full of love, then success and money will find you. This is because manifestations of abundance gather around love.

As the caretaker sign of families and households, Cancer represents a safe and harmonious home. It will lend you great power when you wish for happiness not only for yourself but also for family, friends, and the people around you. So why not entrust to it your vision of your happiest family life?

If you have a problem within your household that you want to resolve, use a Cancer Full Moon Power Wish to your advantage. If your relationship with your child, parent, or spouse feels strained, or if there's a troublemaker in your household, a Cancer Full Moon is the time for you to visualize your family living in peace and harmony, with all these issues resolved. Write your thoughts of gratitude on top of that, and the gentle energy of Cancer is sure to give you a hand.

Cancer New Moon Power Wish

Late June to Late July

A Cancer New Moon helps you . . .

+ Have a fulfilling family life
+ Strengthen family ties
+ Improve parent-child relationships, especially with the mother
+ Be blessed with a child; become pregnant
+ Have control over your emotions
+ Enjoy a fulfilling personal life
+ Create an environment that feels safe
+ Make new friends who are as close to you as your family
+ Purchase the home of your dreams

✦ With anything related to the chest and breasts

Inquiries from the Universe

To help you find clues when you don't know what to write

✦ What is your idea of a happy family?
✦ What is your ideal parent-child relationship like?
✦ How would you like to raise your children?
✦ If you were to work from home, what would that look like?
✦ If you were to build a new home, what would it be like?

TOP 3 POWER WISH EXAMPLES THAT ARE LIKELY TO COME TRUE WITH A CANCER NEW MOON

1. <u>I intend to</u> build a loving, happy family with Frankie.
2. <u>I intend to</u> create a fun family with my partner and two children, living a life full of laughter together.
3. <u>I intend to</u> purchase a piece of land near the ocean within a year and build a house with a balcony.

RECOMMENDED KEYWORDS FOR CANCER POWER WISHES

⚷ *Family*

parent-child, clan, extended family, kin, kindred spirits, best friend, childhood friend, family business, subsidiary, pregnancy, childbirth, kids, parenting, discipline

Residence

home, apartment, second home, renovation, interior, relocate, replace, roommate/housemate, house share

Personal life

after work, safety, recharge, moonlight bath, relax, lifestyle, creature comforts

Cooking

food, recipe, nutrition, table, kitchen, meal

Kind

loving, friendly, full of love, warm, relatable, favorable, approachable

---

⚬ *Take care of*

nurture, protect, help, be kind, be on their side, lend a hand, get in touch with, envelop, unite, join together, support each other, understand (someone), relate, interact, appreciate, sympathize, care for

---

ROMANTIC RELATIONSHIPS AND PARTNERSHIPS

+ I intend to meet a cheerful and kind partner who can get along with my parents.

+ I intend for Frankie's parents to like me and approve of our marriage.

CAREER AND BUSINESS

+ I intend to open a cooking school in my home this fall and teach one hundred students within a year.

+ I intend to create a library café where moms with children can gather.

FINANCES

+ I intend to earn a generous income that allows me to easily give my parents a monthly allowance of two thousand dollars.

+ I intend to double my income so that I can provide my children with the best education.

HABITS

+ I intend to meet up with my spouse's parents for a meal every month and maintain a good relationship with them.

+ I intend to cook a balanced meal for myself at least three times a week.

PERSONALITY

+ I intend to let go of the habit of trying to micromanage my children.

+ From this day on, I intend to convey words of gratitude and caring to my parents without feeling embarrassed.

HEALTH AND BEAUTY

✦ I intend to do thirty push-ups every day, building beautiful and firm pectoral muscles.

✦ I intend to regularly go to an outdoor bath to soak up the moonlight, fully receiving the power of the Moon.

MISCELLANEOUS

✦ I intend to work with my partner to have a baby and share with others the happy news.

✦ I intend to make time for myself at least once a week and become myself again while caring for my father.

Cancer Full Moon Power Wish

Late December to Late January

The themes and keywords are the same as those for the New Moon. Additionally, a Cancer Full Moon helps you release . . .

+ Worrying, meddling, micromanaging
+ Emotional ups and downs, being hypersensitive or fearful
+ Troubles or worries about the chest or breasts

TOP 2 POWER/RELEASE WISH
EXAMPLES THAT ARE LIKELY
TO COME TRUE WITH A CANCER
FULL MOON

1. I found my ideal condo in Chelsea, the neigh-borhood of my dreams. <u>I can't believe I get to live there! Thank you so much.</u>
2. The days of being wrapped up in my emotions are long past. <u>It's amazing that</u> I can just hit the reset button and feel better in a day! <u>Thank you so much.</u>

ROMANTIC RELATIONSHIPS AND PARTNERSHIPS

✦ My son has given me his blessings to marry Frankie! I am so glad he'll have a new dad. Thank you so much.

CAREER AND BUSINESS

✦ As I see the employees I've trained working and suc-ceeding, I feel blessed to be a coach. I am so happy with this job. Thank you so much.

FINANCES

+ I am delightfully surprised that my hobby of baking is bringing in unexpected income. Heartfelt gratitude to my customers! Thank you so much.

HABITS

+ Since I started going to cooking school, I'm more aware of what I eat. It helps me stay healthy—a big plus! Thank you so much.

PERSONALITY

+ My habit of taking out my anger on my children is gone. I no longer lapse into self-hatred, and I feel peaceful every day. Thank you so much.

HEALTH AND BEAUTY

+ Since I started setting the table and eating mindfully, I am no longer eating more than I need. I feel joy in my daily life, and my emotions have evened out dramatically. Thank you so much!

MISCELLANEOUS

✦ My friend introduced me to the perfect roommate! He is so fun and optimistic; I feel comfortable around him, like we've been best friends our whole lives. He's also a great cook! I am so grateful for this miraculous encounter. Thank you so much!

5

New Moon and Full Moon In

LEO

BE A CONFIDENT HERO

Leo Power Wishes

Learn the pleasure and joy of life with the
New Moon.

Eliminate low self-esteem with the Full Moon.

Are you enjoying your life right now? Can you feel from the bottom of your heart that you are happy to be alive? If your answer to both of these questions is no, then make the shift to a life of joy using Leo Power Wishes.

Enjoying your life is neither selfish nor self-indulgent—it is simply necessary in order for your wishes to come true. Wishes don't come true when you're furrowing your brow; they come true naturally as you enjoy life and radiate a happy and fun vibration.

Having fun while manifesting your wishes—Leo helps you make that a reality. The trick with Leo Power Wishes is to set aside obligations and responsibilities and write down what excites you and makes your heart dance—the kind of wish that, if it comes true, will allow you to shine more brightly than ever before. If you have no idea what excites you or what you want to do, you can write a Power Wish that will help you find out.

Romance is included in what excites us, of course. So if you are dying to meet someone and fall in love, you will experience the amazing difference the Leo Power Wishes can make.

Leo Power Wishes are also very helpful if you want to become famous or step into the limelight. They are particularly effective if you have a competition or an audition coming up.

On the other hand, if you have stage fright or aren't great at self-promoting, take advantage of the Full Moon in Leo. Visualize yourself standing tall in the spotlight as you write Power Wishes that praise and celebrate you.

Leo New Moon Power Wish

Late July to Late August

A Leo New Moon helps you . . .

+ Create the life you want
+ Live boldly and confidently
+ Transform an inferiority complex into an appreciation of your own uniqueness
+ Become a great self-promoter
+ Garner attention and acclaim
+ Live a luxurious life
+ Turn hobbies and things you love into something you get paid for
+ Spice up a monotonous life
+ Lead a team or company
+ Succeed in the entertainment industry

✦ With anything related to the heart, back, posture, or circulation

Inquiries from the Universe

To help you find clues when you don't know what to write

✦ In what field would you like to shine?
✦ How would you introduce yourself?
✦ What is your greatest asset?
✦ If you have low self-esteem, why?
✦ What would you do if you could take a month off from work?

TOP 3 POWER WISH EXAMPLES THAT ARE LIKELY TO COME TRUE WITH A LEO NEW MOON

1. From this day on, <u>I intend to</u> make pleasure a priority in my life over obligations and responsibilities.
2. <u>I intend to</u> emphasize my best features and live confidently.
3. <u>I intend to</u> be assigned a new role that allows me to fully shine at my company.

RECOMMENDED KEYWORDS FOR LEO POWER WISHES

⚷ *Uniqueness*

asset, best feature, self-expression, identity, self-image, pride, dignity, self-esteem, originality, creativity, lottery, gamble

⚷ *Aura*

confidence, shine, success, smile, central figure, VIP, celebrity, fame, famous person, acclaim, public figure, dramatic, royal, royalty, privilege, symbol

⚷ *Joy*

be moved, be touched, drama, romance, party, cheerfulness, innocence, fun

⚷ *Star*

hero/heroine, charisma, flamboyant, gorgeous, presence, stage, actor/actress, singer, talent, theater, musical, audition, contest, event, performance

⚷ *Standing tall*

confidently, boldly, cheerfully, extravagantly, without hesitation, fairly and squarely, remarkably, movingly

---

☒—✦ *Be noticed*

be praised, be respected, make a name, take center stage, get up in front of others, be confident, be expressive, promote

---

ROMANTIC RELATIONSHIPS AND PARTNERSHIPS

✦ This summer, I intend to meet someone with a gorgeous smile and to fall passionately in love.

✦ I intend for Noah to propose in a dramatic way when we go on our date next weekend.

CAREER AND BUSINESS

✦ I intend to see my job as a form of self-expression, in which I can work hard to show off my best self.

✦ I intend to nail the final callback audition on November 2 and debut as a stage actor with a major theater company.

✦ I intend to give a stellar presentation that moves the audience at tomorrow's meeting.

✦ I intend to transition to a life in which the more fun I have, the more money I make.

FINANCES

✦ I intend to receive a far bigger bonus than I expected and use the money to go see musicals in New York this June.

✦ I intend to experience firsthand the principle "The more fun I have, the more money I get."

HABITS

✦ I intend to be the hero of my own dramatic life.

✦ I intend to become a person who can declare with confidence that I can create my own fortune and life.

PERSONALITY

✦ I intend to gain the strength and confidence to clearly say what I want to say no matter whom I am speaking with.

✦ I intend to be a fair and square person who can make sound judgments at all times.

HEALTH AND BEAUTY

- ✦ I intend to work to maintain a beautiful posture.
- ✦ I intend to get in shape by going to the gym regularly and doing exercises that raise my heart rate.

MISCELLANEOUS

- ✦ From this day on, I intend to choose an exciting life and live dramatically.
- ✦ I intend to attract attention with my current work and become famous.

Leo Full Moon Power Wish

Late January to Late February

The themes and keywords are the same as those for the New Moon. Additionally, a Leo Full Moon helps you release . . .

+ Being vain, arrogant, or overbearing
+ Low self-esteem, self-denial, undervaluing
+ Troubles or worries about the heart, back, circulation, or posture

---

TOP 2 POWER/RELEASE WISH
EXAMPLES THAT ARE LIKELY TO
COME TRUE WITH A LEO FULL MOON

1. I am fully expressing my unique charm at my new job. <u>My self-esteem has skyrocketed, too. Thank you so much.</u>

2. My negative thoughts and judgments about myself have disappeared completely. <u>Even the inferiority complex I used to have has now turned into confidence! Thank you so much.</u>

ROMANTIC RELATIONSHIPS AND PARTNERSHIPS

+ Sam, the man of my dreams, asked me out on a date. I'm over the Moon! Thank you so much.

CAREER AND BUSINESS

+ Every day I do what I love to do, which is draw, and I'm getting paid for it to boot. How lucky am I? Thank you so much.

FINANCES

✦ I started taking only jobs that I enjoy doing, and now my income has doubled. I've proved to myself that the source of money is joy. Thank you so much.

HABITS

✦ My habit of constant self-deprecation has completely fallen away. My new habit is to whisper to myself, "I'm awesome!" Thank you so much.

PERSONALITY

✦ Since I realized that my smile is my greatest asset, I feel so much more self-assured and have been able to act with confidence no matter where I am or whom I'm with. It feels like a lifetime ago that I used to have social anxiety going to parties. Thank you so much.

HEALTH AND BEAUTY

✦ After getting a professional makeup consultation, I look so fabulous I can hardly recognize myself! My self-esteem has skyrocketed; I'm blown away by my own transformation. Thank you so much!

MISCELLANEOUS

✦ Being with Taylor has helped me see myself in a new way, and my self-image has dramatically improved. Not only am I meeting great people, I'm also making more money than I ever have! I am so grateful to have Taylor in my life. Thank you so much!

6

New Moon and Full Moon In

VIRGO

CULTIVATE AN
ENVIRONMENT THAT
FOSTERS GOOD FORTUNE

Virgo Power Wishes

Form new habits that attract good fortune with
the New Moon.

Sever ties with anything that lowers your vibration with the Full Moon.

Virgo is the sole "regulator" among the twelve signs of
the zodiac. Its role is to properly tidy up anything that
is in disarray, in confusion, or not functioning smoothly,
whether it's work, relationships, or emotions.

Improving health and lifestyle habits in particular is Virgo's specialty. Being healthy and keeping your body in good
condition are prerequisites for attracting opportunities.

When you investigate why someone's wishes aren't coming true, more often than not, they're not taking care of

themselves. They may be habitually neglecting their bodies or not eating well.

That said, humans are creatures of habit. Once something becomes a habit, I know it's difficult to change it.

And that's where Virgo Power Wishes come in! When you rely on a New Moon or Full Moon in Virgo, you'll be surprised by how easily you can quit habits that aren't serving you. You may find yourself with no more urges to smoke or cravings for junk food.

This is because Virgo's energy helps to eliminate what's not needed. I often recommend using Virgo Power Wishes for dieting; both the Full Moon and New Moon are effective for this.

Virgo helps you regulate not only your physical health but also your mental and emotional health. If you are struggling to let go of psychological trauma or negative emotions, use a Virgo Full Moon Power Wish to release them.

Virgo New Moon Power Wish

Late August to Late September

A Virgo New Moon helps you . . .

+ Get your work done quickly
+ Fulfill the role that is required of you
+ Gain recognition and trust from others
+ Skillfully support your superiors
+ Elevate things to the level of perfection
+ Take the best course of action for a situation
+ Make it a habit to declutter and tidy up
+ Take good care of yourself and get back into your groove
+ Improve your physical condition
+ Achieve a healthy weight
+ Succeed in the medical, health care, or healing arts fields

✦ With anything related to the stomach, intestines, and digestion

Inquiries from the Universe

To help you find clues when you don't know what to write

✦ In what ways would you like to be of service to others?
✦ What are your strengths?
✦ What is something that you tend to neglect?
✦ What concerns you in terms of your health?
✦ How would you like to take better care of yourself?

TOP 3 POWER WISH EXAMPLES THAT ARE LIKELY TO COME TRUE WITH A VIRGO NEW MOON

1. <u>I intend to</u> finish my daily desk work in the morning and focus on sales in the afternoon.
2. <u>I intend to</u> offer thoughtful and skilled support to my boss at all times.
3. <u>I intend to</u> eat better and improve my health.

RECOMMENDED KEYWORDS FOR VIRGO POWER WISHES

⚷ *Service*

support, attentive, assistant, secretary, office, work, role, duty, responsibility, delegate

⚷ *Time*

review, regulation, schedule, paperwork, desk work, routine, order, tidying up, decluttering

⚷ *Health-conscious*

stomach, intestines, digestive system, lifestyle habits, taking care of oneself, weight loss, diet, therapy, healing, medicine, medical treatment, alternative medicine, naturopathy, herbs, Chinese herbs, homeopathy, holistic

⚷ *Competent*

management, analysis, organized, efficiency, skill, certification, high level, high standard, meticulous, perfect

⚷ *Pure*

refreshing, well-groomed, dignified, spotless, reserved, sincere, humble, lean, functional, slim

⚷ *Be helpful*

accomplish one's mission, fill a demand, improve, analyze, research, adjust, coordinate, sift through, filter out

ROMANTIC RELATIONSHIPS AND PARTNERSHIPS

+ I intend to support Sam in his life as his best partner.
+ I intend to meet an attractive partner at my new job and for us to become the perfect married couple that everyone envies.

CAREER AND BUSINESS

+ I intend to become a certified herbalist within two years and open up a salon that combines herbal medicine with aromatherapy.
+ I intend to find a new position at a major accounting firm within six months and learn on the job.

FINANCES

+ I intend to get certified in user experience design before the end of the year and get a promotion and a raise.
+ I intend to save seven hundred dollars every month starting this month for my wedding.

HABITS

+ I intend to be more punctual, always operating five minutes ahead of schedule.

+ From this moment on, I intend to swiftly get rid of things I don't use.

PERSONALITY

+ I intend to actively choose what helps me grow in my work and personal life, instead of taking the easy way out.

+ I intend to finish all my work perfectly without cutting corners, no matter how difficult it is.

HEALTH AND BEAUTY

+ I intend to stop snacking on junk food and eat dried fruit and other healthful food instead.

+ I intend to skip dinner on the day of the New Moon every month, giving my stomach a break and bringing my body back into balance.

MISCELLANEOUS

- ✦ I intend to get plenty of sleep, especially when I am busy, keeping my body in optimal condition.
- ✦ I intend to improve my grooming and speech in order to make a good impression on my customers.

Virgo Full Moon Power Wish

Late February to Late March

The themes and keywords are the same as those for the New Moon. Additionally, a Virgo Full Moon helps you release . . .

✦ Being fussy, critical, or negative
✦ An inability to forgive other people's mistakes
✦ An attachment to being perfect
✦ Troubles or worries about the digestive system or weight, constipation, diarrhea

> **TOP 2 POWER/RELEASE WISH EXAMPLES THAT ARE LIKELY TO COME TRUE WITH A VIRGO FULL MOON**
>
> 1. I have completely recovered from "can't-tidy" syndrome! <u>Now my friends can come over anytime. Thank you so much.</u>
> 2. I lost my love handles and now I can easily fit into my clothes. <u>I love that my clothes are even a little loose on me! Thank you so much.</u>

ROMANTIC RELATIONSHIPS AND PARTNERSHIPS

✦ I am building a positive and faithful relationship with Sam. I think he might propose soon! Thank you so much.

CAREER AND BUSINESS

✦ I've become so much more efficient at work ever since I became mindful of how I allocate my time. Thanks to this, I can now make full use of my after-work hours. Thank you so much.

FINANCES

✦ My skills and accomplishments have been recognized, and I've been rewarded with a raise of twelve thousand dollars. I am grateful to my boss, who gave me good reviews. Thank you so much.

HABITS

✦ Lately, I no longer want to smoke cigarettes. Thanks to this, my skin has cleared up and looks brighter! Thank you so much.

PERSONALITY

✦ I honestly believe now that only good can come out of my life. I'm living a stress-free life without needless worries. Thank you so much.

HEALTH AND BEAUTY

✦ Now that I go to work an hour earlier, I never stay up late anymore. I'm keeping regular hours, I'm no longer constipated, and everything is turning around for the better. Thank you so much!

MISCELLANEOUS

+ Since this past spring, all the work and relationships that used to burden me have been naturally falling away. It's as if a huge weight has been lifted. I'm truly content now that I'm in a place where I'm free to go as I please without worrying about anyone else. Thank you so much.

7

New Moon and Full Moon In

LIBRA

MANIFEST THE IDEAL PARTNERSHIP

Libra Power Wishes

Find the perfect partner with the New Moon.

Let go of futile relationships with the Full Moon.

I bet there's no one out there who hasn't wished to meet their ideal partner or find their soul mate. Life can change greatly depending on whom you meet. It's not far-fetched to say that life is about whom you end up with.

When we meet someone, it's really destiny—in a realm beyond our control. At the same time, we're not completely powerless, either.

If you want to meet people, Libra Power Wishes are at your service. Libra takes care of all romantic relationships, from first encounters to courtship to marriage. Whereas

Cancer rules marriage in a broader sense, including family relationships, Libra focuses on marriage as a partnership—the one-on-one relationship between the couple.

When the New Moon or Full Moon is in Libra, you can make all kinds of Power Wishes pertaining to marriage, whether it's meeting a soul mate, taking your relationship to the next level, or being proposed to by the partner of your dreams.

Getting into the visuals can also be helpful here—perhaps you'd love to wear a mermaid wedding dress, or go to Majorca for your honeymoon. With Libra, the more you visualize your wish, the more easily it comes true, so go ahead and imagine the most romantic situations you can think of.

If you'd like to end a current relationship or let go of unrequited love, or if you're seeking a divorce, make good use of the Libra Full Moon Power Wish.

Libra Power Wishes are also effective for business contracts and partnerships.

Libra New Moon Power Wish

Late September to Late October

A Libra New Moon helps you . . .

- ✦ Begin a new relationship
- ✦ Meet a potential romantic partner
- ✦ Become closer with your love interest
- ✦ Get engaged or married
- ✦ Improve all relationships
- ✦ Find a good business partner
- ✦ Sign a contract on favorable terms
- ✦ Win a lawsuit or a trial
- ✦ Become more likable and popular
- ✦ No longer feel intimidated in public

✦ With anything related to the waist and lower back

Inquiries from the Universe

To help you find clues when you don't know what to write

✦ What kind of man or woman do you long to be loved by?

✦ What do you look for in a partner?

✦ What are the things you want to improve in your relationships?

✦ What aspects of yourself feel unbalanced to you?

✦ What parts of your appearance would you like to improve?

TOP 3 POWER WISH EXAMPLES THAT ARE LIKELY TO COME TRUE WITH A LIBRA NEW MOON

1. <u>I intend to</u> meet my soul mate and begin my new life very soon.
2. <u>I intend to</u> build comfortable relationships with every person I interact with day-to-day.
3. <u>I intend to</u> become an elegant, sophisticated person who makes a good impression on everyone.

RECOMMENDED KEYWORDS FOR LIBRA POWER WISHES

Marriage

romance, engagement, betrothal, get married, wedding, partner, soul mate, engagement ring, wedding dress, tuxedo

⚷ Relationships

courtship, social, business partner, soul mate, business partnership, collaboration, connection, contract

⚷ Peace

love, harmony, agreement, mediation, win-win, fair, balance, manners, etiquette

⚷ Beauty

looks, appearance, first impression, vibe, hair and makeup, fashion, figure, beauty salon

⚷ Sophisticated

elegant, stylish, flawless, clever, good taste, considerate, empathic, get along with everyone

⚷ Encounter

go out with, date, ask out, swoon, love, attracted to, captivated by, fall in love, confess your love

ROMANTIC RELATIONSHIPS AND PARTNERSHIPS

- ✦ I intend to meet my soul mate and get married at the perfect time.
- ✦ I intend to talk about marriage with Madison and for us to meet each other's parents before the end of this year.

CAREER AND BUSINESS

- ✦ I intend to be blessed with the most amazing co-workers and enjoy working with them in harmony every day.
- ✦ I intend to find a manufacturer that meets my requirements perfectly and release my new product by the end of the year.

FINANCES

- ✦ I intend to work in a stylish setting while receiving plenty of income.
- ✦ I intend to reach an agreement with the president of my company in order for my monthly salary

to increase by one thousand dollars starting next month.

HABITS

+ I intend to make it a habit to smile whenever my eyes meet someone else's.
+ I intend to develop an eye for beauty by visiting museums and art galleries on the weekends.

PERSONALITY

+ I intend to get along with everyone without being shy.
+ I intend to listen to different opinions instead of being attached to my own.

HEALTH AND BEAUTY

+ I intend to take Pilates and ballet classes every week, toning my core and building a body that is balanced between strong and elegant.
+ I intend to work with a personal stylist to do a makeup and wardrobe makeover, creating a sophisticated, elegant new look.

MISCELLANEOUS

+ I intend to work on my posture and become elegant and sophisticated.
+ I intend to fully enjoy my time at work and at home, achieving a perfect work-life balance.

Libra Full Moon Power Wish

Late March to Late April

The themes and keywords are the same as those for the New Moon. Additionally, a Libra Full Moon helps you release . . .

+ Indecisiveness, people-pleasing, or not being able to say no
+ An inability to make your own decisions; being dependent on others
+ Troubles or worries about the waist and lower back

TOP 2 POWER/RELEASE WISH EXAMPLES THAT ARE LIKELY TO COME TRUE WITH A LIBRA FULL MOON

1. I'm currently going out with the woman I met the other day. It looks like she may be <u>meeting my parents next month. Thank you so much.</u>

2. I can now politely say no when I'm asked to do something I don't want to do. Thanks to this, I'm no longer stressed, and <u>life feels easier. Thank you so much.</u>

ROMANTIC RELATIONSHIPS AND PARTNERSHIPS

✦ I was able to make a clean break from my dead-end relationship with Sean. Now I wish him all the best. Thank you so much.

CAREER AND BUSINESS

✦ I signed a stylist contract with a fashion magazine. Words can't describe how happy I am! Thank you so much.

FINANCES

✦ I am earning enough money to buy all the clothes I want and still have money left. It's wonderful to be able to dress the way I want. Thank you so much, truly.

HABITS

✦ Thanks to the ballroom dance lessons I started taking, I no longer spend my weekends on the couch. My body is getting in shape, too! Thank you so much.

PERSONALITY

✦ The social anxiety I used to have is fading away. I'm learning how to socialize like a grown-up now. Thank you so much.

HEALTH AND BEAUTY

✦ I swapped my desk chair for a balance ball, and now I have more definition around my waist and hips. My upper and lower body look much more in proportion. Sweet! Thank you so much.

MISCELLANEOUS

✦ Whether it's love, career, money, passion, health, or relationships, I'm feeling fulfilled in every area of my life. I'm giving a toast to my own amazing life! Thank you so much.

8

New Moon and Full Moon In

SCORPIO

ENJOY YOUR OWN
TRANSFORMATION

Scorpio Power Wishes

> Challenge yourself to an alluring transformation
> with the New Moon.
>
> Say goodbye to your past self with the Full Moon.

Scorpio may be a bit difficult to grasp. Life and death, resurrection and restoration, sex and sexuality—Scorpio governs themes that are, in a way, extremely heavy. Since these themes often can't be discussed lightly, you may feel a little reluctant to write a Power Wish about them.

That said, Scorpio's ruler is Pluto—the most powerful celestial body in the solar system. By using Scorpio Power Wishes skillfully, you can turn your life around 180 degrees. If your desire is to be reborn and start a brand-new life, there's nothing more potent than a Scorpio Power Wish.

What I'd like you to remember is that Scorpio has the power to transform things. *Change* is too lukewarm a word to describe its truly transformational power. If you are seeking something totally different from the status quo or looking to resurrect what has been ruined, Scorpio Power Wishes are your greatest tool.

Scorpio, along with Taurus, is a sign that means money. It rules money at the asset level, such as real estate, stocks, and savings, as well as passive income such as royalties. With Scorpio, it would be more effective to write a Power Wish about increasing your net worth rather than about just having more income.

Romantic relationships are also among the themes of Scorpio, though more in the sense of soul-to-soul connections than marriage. We can say that soul mates, in the truest sense of the term, are in Scorpio's domain.

Scorpio also governs sex and hormones, so if you want to boost your sex appeal, Scorpio Power Wishes can make it happen.

Scorpio New Moon Power Wish

Late October to Late November

A Scorpio New Moon helps you . . .

+ Focus on one thing at a deeper level
+ Demonstrate outstanding focus
+ Deepen your bond with a loved one
+ Attract a soul mate
+ Turn around a hopeless situation
+ Restore or resurrect what has been ruined
+ Turn a past mistake into a success
+ Achieve a stunning transformation
+ Purchase real estate
+ Gain passive income

❧

- ✦ With anything related to the uterus, ovaries, sexual organs, urinary organs, and menstruation
- ✦ With anything related to hormones, sexuality, and anti-aging

Inquiries from the Universe

To help you find clues when you don't know what to write

- ✦ What mission would you like to dedicate your life to?
- ✦ What situation would you like to turn around?
- ✦ If you were to be reborn right now, what kind of person would you like to be?
- ✦ What is something that didn't go well in the past that you'd like to give another try?
- ✦ What kind of real estate would you like to own, and where?

TOP 3 POWER WISH EXAMPLES THAT ARE LIKELY TO COME TRUE WITH A SCORPIO NEW MOON

1. <u>I intend to</u> part with my past self and begin a completely new life.
2. <u>I intend to</u> share the rest of my life with a soul mate.
3. <u>I intend to</u> take this New Moon as an opportunity to get out of my rut and ride a wave of good fortune.

RECOMMENDED KEYWORDS FOR SCORPIO POWER WISHES

⚷ *Restoration*

resurrection, transformation, reset, recharge, meditation, underlying strength, faith, focus, essence, value, truth, honest feelings, fresh start, comeback, try again, instinct

⚷ *Soul mate*

destiny, better half, past life, karma, ancestor, heredity, DNA, life partner, adoption, sex

⚷ *Income*

asset, inheritance, bank, insurance, stock, investment, real estate, royalty, passive income, finance, life's work

⚷ *Mysterious*

sexy, sex appeal, alluring, hidden, lingerie, the other side, secret art, psychic powers, charisma

⚷ One and only

unshakable, true, uncompromising, nowhere else,
rare, precious, in the know, astronomical, at the
soul level, fated

⚷ Belong together

deepen a relationship, understand each other, remarry, see through, commit, share, inherit, take
over, bequeath

ROMANTIC RELATIONSHIPS AND PARTNERSHIPS

+ I intend to meet my soul mate and establish a bond
that transcends time and space.

+ I intend to meet a sexy partner and remarry within a
year.

CAREER AND BUSINESS

+ I intend to fully master my current job and become a charismatic leading figure in the field of couples counseling.

+ I intend to find a job that I can call my life's purpose and devote the rest of my life to meaningful work.

FINANCES

+ I intend to find a second job and purchase a penthouse with a view of Central Park.

+ I intend to compose numerous hit songs and live comfortably on royalties for the rest of my life.

HABITS

+ I intend to donate 10 percent of all unexpected income and bonuses to charity.

+ I intend to make a habit of meditating before bed, preparing myself to sleep soundly.

PERSONALITY

- ✦ I intend to live with my eyes on the future, without being dragged down by the past.
- ✦ I intend to allow the talent and genes I inherited from my family to fully blossom in my life.

HEALTH AND BEAUTY

- ✦ I intend to do mindfulness meditation every night before bed, developing the mental strength to fully restore myself overnight even if I have had a bad day.
- ✦ I intend to focus on rehab after my surgery this winter and return to work fully recovered in the spring.

MISCELLANEOUS

- ✦ I intend to use my feelings of regret and frustration as a springboard to give myself a fresh start as I tackle a new project.
- ✦ I intend to embrace my own beauty and be ready to fall in love at any time.

Scorpio Full Moon Power Wish

Late April to Late May

The themes and keywords are the same as those for the New Moon. Additionally, a Scorpio Full Moon helps you release . . .

+ Feelings of paranoia, pessimism, and closed-mindedness
+ Resentment, vengeance, jealousy, and attachment
+ Troubles or worries about the uterus, ovaries, sexual organs, urinary organs, or menstruation

TOP 2 POWER/RELEASE WISH
EXAMPLES THAT ARE LIKELY
TO COME TRUE WITH A SCORPIO
FULL MOON

1. The irrational belief that I'll never be loved by the one I love has disappeared completely. <u>I am going to live with a positive attitude from now on! Thank you so much.</u>

2. This Full Moon brought on a complete break-through for me! I can feel this powerful energy welling up inside me like hot lava. <u>I'm going to make a stunning comeback now! Thank you so much!</u>

ROMANTIC RELATIONSHIPS AND PARTNERSHIPS

✦ Sam and I had been best friends but not quite lovers, but now our relationship has deepened, and we have made a commitment to each other. I feel a huge sense of relief now that I'm with the partner I was destined to be with. Thank you so much.

CAREER AND BUSINESS

✦ I gave myself a fresh start with a new business, and now it's bringing far more revenue than I ever expected. I'm so glad I took a leap of faith! Thank you so much.

FINANCES

✦ I met a trustworthy financial planner who taught me the ins and outs of real estate management. Passive income is about to become a reality! Thank you so much.

HABITS

✦ Ever since I made a habit of doing breathing exercises before bed, my insomnia has disappeared. I wake up feeling so refreshed now! Thank you so much.

PERSONALITY

✦ All the grudges and grievances I was holding against my ex have disappeared like magic. I am grateful for the time we shared together. Thank you so much.

HEALTH AND BEAUTY

✦ My new partner and I have the best sexual chemistry! I feel whole and complete both physically and emotionally. My body has never been healthier, and I feel a sense of safety and happiness that I've never experienced before. Thank you so much.

MISCELLANEOUS

✦ My spouse and I were finally able to adopt a beautiful boy! We both instinctively knew he was the one the moment we first saw him at the foster home. I can't wait to celebrate Christmas with the three of us. Thank you so much.

9

New Moon and Full Moon In

SAGITTARIUS

PURSUE ENDLESS POSSIBILITIES

Sagittarius Power Wishes

Dive into the unknown with the New Moon.

Remove any unnecessary hindrance with the Full Moon.

The other day I was asked, "What do people whose wishes easily come true have in common?" I answered, "They are optimistic." Having an optimistic outlook on life is the first prerequisite for your wish coming true. Why? Because everything that happens around you is the projection of your own consciousness.

Neither good fortune nor coincidence determines whether your wish comes true—it's all about the state of your consciousness.

Being optimistic means interpreting all situations positively and envisioning a bright future. And the sign that helps us cultivate this consciousness is Sagittarius.

Sagittarius provides us with endless possibilities and numerous opportunities. Only Sagittarius, with the "lucky star" Jupiter as its ruler, gifts us with amazing opportunities that feel like windfalls. It's quite a generous sign, so instead of getting pessimistic and assuming your wishes are unrealistic (Sagittarius hates pessimism above all else), go ahead and ask for everything and anything you want.

When it comes to a Sagittarius Power Wish, whatever your wish is, make it *big*. If you get too humble or settle for a wish that feels reasonable, you're letting the power of Sagittarius go to waste. With Sagittarius, you have to go for the highest and biggest—the absolute best outcome you can imagine.

If you tend to think negatively, use a Sagittarius Full Moon Power Wish to let that go completely.

Sagittarius is also associated with overseas. If you're looking to expand internationally or have a wish pertaining to foreign countries, be sure to make a global-scale Power Wish with Sagittarius.

Sagittarius New Moon Power Wish

Late November to Late December

A Sagittarius New Moon helps you . . .

+ Expand or develop what's currently there
+ Attract opportunities and possibilities
+ Get timely help even if you're in crisis
+ Live and act optimistically and joyfully
+ Achieve above-average results in all things
+ Have good fortune by default
+ Open up and become extroverted
+ Make international connections
+ Enjoy a career that spans the globe
+ Succeed in the fields of mass media, publishing, and law

✦ With anything related to the hips and thighs

Inquiries from the Universe

To help you find clues when you don't know what to write

✦ If you had total freedom, what would you like to do?
✦ What is holding you back?
✦ Why haven't you put your ideas into action?
✦ What would you like to expand or develop?
✦ If you were to have a whole month off, where would you like to go?

TOP 3 POWER WISH EXAMPLES THAT ARE LIKELY TO COME TRUE WITH A SAGITTARIUS NEW MOON

1. <u>I intend to</u> trust my good fortune and achieve all the success I want.
2. <u>I intend to</u> prioritize hope and possibility over fear or anxiety.
3. <u>I intend to</u> travel around the world and live freely.

RECOMMENDED KEYWORDS FOR SAGITTARIUS POWER WISHES

Freedom

travel, action, adventure, outdoors, target, goal, a new world, the unknown, overseas, possibility

⚷ *Optimistic*

generous, tolerant, magnanimous, bold, open, extroverted, joyful, windfall, good fortune, luck, lucky, fortunate

⚷ *Inquisitiveness*

professional training, graduate school, MBA, degree, master, doctor, master's degree program, doctoral program, international, worldwide, bilingual, academic

⚷ *Authentic*

carefree, genuine, straightforward, as is, relaxed, natural, healthy, up-front

⚷ *Frankly*

freely, as I please, straightforwardly, positively, with ease, naturally, as swift as an arrow, quickly, in a natural way, comfortably

> ⚏—⊕ *Dive in*
>
> try, take risks, give it a go, go well, develop, grow,
> increase, widen, expand, be liberated, run through,
> fly away

ROMANTIC RELATIONSHIPS AND PARTNERSHIPS

+ I intend to be happy and relaxed around Frankie instead of getting nervous.
+ I intend to marry an Italian and live in Rome or Milan.

CAREER AND BUSINESS

+ I intend to keep my eyes on not only my home country but also the rest of the world by working and succeeding globally.
+ I intend to expand my possibilities by trying out jobs I have no experience in.

FINANCES

✦ I intend to steadily bring in more than fifteen thousand dollars every month as a travel journalist.

✦ After I finish studying abroad, I intend to find a new job at a multinational company and double my annual income.

HABITS

✦ I intend to stay centered in times of crisis.

✦ From now on, I intend to see my life as an adventure and stride through it boldly.

PERSONALITY

✦ I intend to respect views that are different from mine and keep my mind open to all things.

✦ Whenever problems arise, I intend to see them positively as games worth playing.

HEALTH AND BEAUTY

✦ I intend to tone my hips with horseback riding lessons twice a month.

✦ I intend to stop going to bed late and begin living a healthier lifestyle.

MISCELLANEOUS

✦ I intend to start taking French classes this month and master everyday conversations within a year.

✦ I intend to publish a how-to book about glamping within a year and make it a bestseller.

Sagittarius Full Moon Power Wish

Late May to Late June

The themes and keywords are the same as those for the New Moon. Additionally, a Sagittarius Full Moon helps you release . . .

+ Being irresponsible, flaky, careless, or deceptive
+ Being ambiguous, incomplete, or not thorough
+ Troubles and worries about the lower back, hips, and thighs

TOP 2 POWER/RELEASE WISH
EXAMPLES THAT ARE LIKELY TO
COME TRUE WITH A SAGITTARIUS
FULL MOON

1. I have total faith that my possibilities are end-less. I am now going to <u>make all my dreams come true! Thank you so much.</u>
2. I am having fun consciously trying things that used to feel difficult for me. <u>It feels so good</u> to overcome the things I couldn't do before. <u>Thank you so much.</u>

ROMANTIC RELATIONSHIPS AND PARTNERSHIPS

◆ Frankie has such a big heart; he is the man of my dreams. I am so grateful to have met him. Thank you so much.

CAREER AND BUSINESS

✦ I'm getting transferred to my dream branch in New York! Words can't express how happy I am. It's a dream come true. Thank you so much!

FINANCES

✦ I successfully acquired new clients this month, and my sales skyrocketed. It's all going according to plan. Thank you so much.

HABITS

✦ Ever since I made a habit of not making any plans for the weekend, I've been experiencing interesting synchronicities one after another. I'm totally in the flow right now! Thank you so much.

PERSONALITY

✦ I no longer abandon work halfway through, and I've been able to produce solid results. I'm getting great feedback from my boss, too. Thank you so much.

HEALTH AND BEAUTY

✦ I am enjoying my ideal lifestyle of working in the city during the week and spending the weekend at my cabin in the Catskills. Being surrounded by nature beats any health regimen or supplement for me. Thank you so much.

MISCELLANEOUS

✦ Thanks to my boss recognizing my personality and skills, it was so easy for me to get my green card. I can't believe how quickly it happened! I am so grateful for her generosity and support. Thank you so much.

10

New Moon and Full Moon In

CAPRICORN

ACHIEVE SUCCESS AND HIGHER STATUS

Capricorn Power Wishes

Achieve the exact success you want with the New Moon.

Let go of shakiness and uncertainty with the Full Moon.

Capricorn is all about getting results. Its mission is to achieve and gain prestige.

If you have a numerical goal that you want to attain or a project that you want to succeed, manifest your desired results by using Capricorn Power Wishes.

No matter how hard you work, it's all for nothing unless you produce results that others recognize—that's the Capricorn mind-set. So of course when you write a Capricorn

Power Wish, it's important to describe your desired outcome as clearly as possible. It's even more effective if you include specific numbers, such as "50 percent higher," "ten thousand dollars," or "number one in sales."

When it comes to anything work-related, nothing beats Capricorn Power Wishes! They will help you achieve all kinds of career success, from great reviews to promotions to raises.

Since Capricorn is deeply tied to public entities such as countries and governments, it's a piece of cake for Capricorn to support you in passing exams or getting a certification or license from the government. In particular, if you are seeking success in the role of a teacher or manager, Capricorn Power Wishes are your greatest tool.

Capricorn does tend to focus on work, but it's not entirely powerless when it comes to your personal life. If you want to marry someone who is much older than you or is of high status, a Capricorn Power Wish can be a powerful ally. It's also a good idea to get help from Capricorn when you want to be with someone who is honest, sincere, and down-to-earth.

Capricorn New Moon Power Wish

Late December to Late January

A Capricorn New Moon helps you . . .

+ Achieve a big goal
+ Make steady efforts without giving up halfway
+ Get increasingly recognized and receive a promotion or raise
+ Become the leading authority or the foremost figure in your field
+ Earn the approval of your superiors and be chosen for a role
+ Move up to a higher status
+ Eliminate everything that is excessive or unnecessary
+ Improve relationships with your father or your boss
+ Marry a successful person of high status
+ Begin a romantic relationship with marriage in mind

❦

✦ With anything related to the teeth, bones, joints, or skin

Inquiries from the Universe

To help you find clues when you don't know what to write

✦ In what field would you like to work and succeed?
✦ What is your ultimate goal in life?
✦ What is something you'd like to accomplish no matter how long it takes?
✦ What is something you have given up on halfway through?
✦ What is something you'd like to quit right now?

TOP 3 POWER WISH EXAMPLES THAT ARE LIKELY TO COME TRUE WITH A CAPRICORN NEW MOON

1. <u>I intend to</u> easily meet this month's sales goals.
2. <u>I intend to</u> produce the best results in everything I do.
3. <u>I intend to</u> study steadily for the GRE and celebrate my success during Christmas.

RECOMMENDED KEYWORDS FOR CAPRICORN POWER WISHES

🔑 *Status*

position, title, honor, glory, award, medal, top-level, be appointed, be chosen, foremost figure

⚷ *Mastery*

training, discipline, teacher, master level, plan, basics, foundation, platform, growth, improvement, achieve a goal

⚷ *Tradition*

the real deal, high quality, royal warrant holder, prestige, formality, long-established shop, distinguished family, background, history, traditional performing arts, orthodox, authority

⚷ *Country*

nation, government, organization, corporation, the public, state license

⚷ *Steadily*

surely, consistently, steadfastly, according to plan, as planned, one step at a time, plug away, taking time, stoically, resolutely, officially, publicly, truly, openly, rightfully, without a doubt, because of hard work

Accomplish

produce results, attain, pass, be recognized, be recommended, get pulled up, get headhunted, get a raise, advance, move up the ladder

ROMANTIC RELATIONSHIPS AND PARTNERSHIPS

+ I intend to patiently build my relationship with Sam one step at a time.
+ I intend to meet a financially secure partner with an established career and build a family together.

CAREER AND BUSINESS

+ I intend to be headhunted by Google within one year and receive an offer that doubles my current salary.
+ I intend to hire a capable right hand and get my business incorporated as quickly as possible.

FINANCES

+ I intend for my efforts and accomplishments this quarter to be recognized and to receive a raise of twenty thousand dollars.

+ I intend to get a new job at a company that appreciates my experience and skills with an annual salary of $150,000 or more.

HABITS

+ I intend to have clear boundaries in my life by focusing on my job during the week and having all the fun I want on weekends.

+ I intend to go for a run on Sundays so that I can start my week with my mind refreshed.

PERSONALITY

+ I intend to set big goals and keep growing without settling for mediocrity.

+ I intend to take my time building a solid foundation and gaining experience, instead of rushing to get results.

HEALTH AND BEAUTY

+ I intend to strengthen my lower body by walking at least thirty minutes every day starting tomorrow.
+ I intend to get my teeth whitened regularly so I can feel confident about my smile.

MISCELLANEOUS

+ I intend to talk to my father more so that our relationship can improve.
+ I intend to tackle my current project seriously so that it becomes a major accomplishment for me.

Capricorn Full Moon Power Wish

Late June to Late July

The themes and keywords are the same as those for the New Moon. Additionally, a Capricorn Full Moon helps you release . . .

- Being inflexible, straitlaced, or dull
- Being apathetic, cold, or unsympathetic
- Troubles and worries about teeth, bones, or skin

> ## TOP 2 POWER/RELEASE WISH EXAMPLES THAT ARE LIKELY TO COME TRUE WITH A CAPRICORN FULL MOON
>
> 1. My efforts thus far have been recognized, and I am getting promoted to regional manager. <u>First goal accomplished! Thank you so much.</u>
> 2. I've completely let go of the anxiety about not seeing any results despite my hard work. I know that the longer it takes, <u>the more I gain. Thank you so much.</u>

ROMANTIC RELATIONSHIPS AND PARTNERSHIPS

+ After steadily deepening my relationship with Frankie, whom I met while studying for the CPA exam, we are now engaged and planning to get married in October. I give thanks from the bottom of my heart for this wonderful encounter with such a sincere partner. Thank you so much.

83

Fullmoon 3.57am
    Taurus

CAREER AND BUSINESS

✦ My company performed far beyond expectations this first year, and we are already net positive. It's all thanks to my staff working so hard. Thank you so much.

FINANCES

✦ I've been making steady progress in my career in the past three years, and my income has been multiplying. I now know for sure that hard work pays off. Thank you so much.

HABITS

✦ I've been visualizing myself succeeding every night as I go to sleep. I am convinced it'll soon become a reality. Thank you so much.

PERSONALITY

✦ I've said goodbye to suppressing my emotions and acting cool. From now on I will express love from my heart! Thank you so much.

HEALTH AND BEAUTY

✦ Thanks to the big raise I got this year, I was able to start the orthodontic treatment to straighten my teeth. I can't wait to see how I'll look six months from now! Thank you so much.

MISCELLANEOUS

✦ I passed the medical licensing examination and have officially become a doctor! I've never been happier in my life. Hooray! Thank you so much!

11

New Moon and Full Moon In

AQUARIUS

BREAK THROUGH THE
STATUS QUO AND ADVANCE
TO THE NEXT LEVEL

Aquarius Power Wishes

Start a revolution in your life with the New Moon.

Enjoy a lifestyle of freedom with the Full Moon.

You've been stuck in a deadlock. You've hit a wall and can't get ahead. You can't find a solution. In these desperate times, Aquarius Power Wishes come to your aid.

Aquarius represents revolution and reform. It is particularly good at stirring things up when there's no movement and creating a new flow. When the New Moon or Full Moon is in Aquarius, you can wish for a breakthrough and expect things to unfold quickly.

As a super progressive sign, Aquarius also goes well with eccentric dreams and outlandish wishes. "I intend for the video I upload on YouTube to get more than a million views and for me to be interviewed by CNN"—even a wish like this, for example, is totally acceptable when it comes to Aquarius Power Wishes. So why not spice things up a bit and include a wish that's as unconventional as this one? After all, the ruler of Aquarius is Uranus, which is known to knock our socks off! Even if it doesn't come true word for word, it's possible for it to lead to unexpected developments.

Another area of Aquarius's expertise is the internet. Representing technology, innovation, and a broad human connection encompassing all ages, genders, and nationalities, Aquarius can be considered the very symbol of the internet age. The New Moon Power Wish is great for launching or growing an online business; the Full Moon Power Wish is a smooth helper for successful social media marketing or going viral.

Aquarius also lends you great power to claim your freedom. When you are yearning to break free of old limitations and live freely, there's nothing more empowering than Aquarius Power Wishes.

Of the twelve zodiac signs, Aquarius is the only one that represents the Universe. With an Aquarius Power Wish, you can therefore effectively ask to catch all the signals from the Universe without fail, or to attract at least one synchronicity per day.

Aquarius New Moon Power Wish

Late January to Late February

An Aquarius New Moon helps you . . .

+ Live a life that is not bound by convention
+ Work and succeed as a freelancer
+ Come up with an ingenious idea
+ Think outside the box
+ Move with the times and achieve success
+ Succeed with an online business
+ Express your creative talent
+ Make new friends and broaden connections
+ Utilize social media effectively
+ Change your life completely

❧

- ✦ With anything related to the calf and ankle
- ✦ With anything related to alternative medicine

Inquiries from the Universe

To help you find clues when you don't know what to write

- ✦ What is something you'd like to change entirely?
- ✦ What kinds of people would you like to connect with?
- ✦ What is the first thing you want to improve in your life?
- ✦ In what ways do you feel bound by convention?
- ✦ How would you like to express your uniqueness?

TOP 3 POWER WISH EXAMPLES THAT ARE LIKELY TO COME TRUE WITH AN AQUARIUS NEW MOON

1. <u>I intend to</u> be brave enough to live freely.
2. <u>I intend to</u> stop living like everyone else and find value in being different.
3. <u>I intend to</u> free myself from the shackles of convention and live the life I truly want.

RECOMMENDED KEYWORDS FOR AQUARIUS POWER WISHES

Network

friend, friendship, best friend, kindred spirit, horizontal connections, comrades, group, freedom, freelance, collaboration

Global

the whole world, philanthropy, long-distance relationship, inspiration, uniqueness, ingenious, innovative, extraordinary, latest

Ecology

Earth, the Universe, planet, astronomy, astrology, signals from the Universe, the environment, alternative medicine, volunteer, nonprofit, conservation

Information technology

internet, social media, system, programming

Logically

objectively, with a broad perspective, calmly, rationally, without worrying about what others think, without being bound by convention, separately, liberally, dramatically, by the roots, boldly, all at once

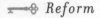 *Reform*

break, override, surpass, adopt, simplify, stream-
line, revamp, transform, reshape, move with the
times, connect, breakthrough

ROMANTIC RELATIONSHIPS AND PARTNERSHIPS

+ Even after Taylor and I get married, I intend for us
  to remain best friends and understand each other
  deeply.

+ I intend for my long-distance relationship with Taylor to deepen the bond between us.

CAREER AND BUSINESS

+ I intend to quit my job at the end of March and succeed as a freelancer.

+ I intend to reserve my routine work for designated
  times so that I have more room in my schedule.

FINANCES

+ I intend to launch an e-commerce business that surpasses two hundred thousand dollars in sales during the first year.

+ I intend to add another digit to my annual income by changing how I think about my work.

HABITS

+ I intend to turn all my inspired ideas into new projects instead of letting them languish.

+ I intend to make new friends with different backgrounds through my monthly volunteer work.

PERSONALITY

+ I intend to keep sharing my opinions and thoughts on social media without worrying about being criticized.

+ Whenever I have to make a difficult decision, I intend to ask myself what serves the world rather than what's profitable.

HEALTH AND BEAUTY

✦ I intend to do thirty calf lifts every morning, building my leg muscles and the strength to complete a full marathon.

✦ I intend to learn qigong and breathing techniques to improve my health without resorting to medication.

MISCELLANEOUS

✦ I intend to study astrology and live in harmony with the Universe.

✦ I intend to start creating my own work instead of waiting for it to show up.

Aquarius Full Moon Power Wish

Late July to Late August

The themes and keywords are the same as those for the New Moon. Additionally, an Aquarius Full Moon helps you release . . .

+ Inability to rely on others; being contentious or self-righteous
+ Repulsion by or rebelliousness toward society or authority
+ Troubles and worries about the calves or ankles

> ## TOP 2 POWER/RELEASE WISH EXAMPLES THAT ARE LIKELY TO COME TRUE WITH AN AQUARIUS FULL MOON
>
> 1. I now receive signals from the Universe and also can understand their meaning. It's so fun to recognize these signals! Thank you so much.
> 2. I've let go of the idea that it's easier to be alone than to be with someone. And now a potential partner has already shown up! Thank you so much.

ROMANTIC RELATIONSHIPS AND PARTNERSHIPS

✦ Taylor and I are enjoying a free and comfortable relationship without trying to control each other. I am grateful for my perfect partner. Thank you so much.

CAREER AND BUSINESS

✦ The green business I've been dreaming of is now taking off for real. It's a miracle how many companies have agreed to sponsor us! Thank you so much.

FINANCES

✦ I now have a free lifestyle with no time constraints, as well as more than enough income. Now that my dream lifestyle has become a reality, I couldn't be happier! Thank you so much.

HABITS

✦ I am no longer in thrall to convention and reputation. Now I want a cutting-edge lifestyle! Thank you so much.

PERSONALITY

✦ I am no longer in the habit of overthinking everything. My life has turned around now that I make inspiration my priority. Thank you so much.

HEALTH AND BEAUTY

✦ The general malaise that hadn't responded to treatment has improved significantly, thanks to my taking dietary supplements to balance out my nutrition. I'm feeling younger and stronger every day! Thank you so much.

MISCELLANEOUS

✦ I now have the fortune and freedom to turn anything I desire into reality. I have no doubts, thanks to the Universe creating the exact synchronicities I need and constantly guiding me to the highest and best. Thank you from the bottom of my heart.

12

New Moon and Full Moon In

PISCES

FORGIVE EVERYTHING
WITH TREMENDOUS LOVE

Pisces Power Wishes

Bring closure to a situation with the New Moon.

Clear out past attachments with the Full Moon.

As the final sign of the zodiac, Pisces represents completion. Since it signifies the ending of a cycle, when it comes to Pisces Power Wishes, it's more appropriate to go for closure and clearing out rather than a new beginning. If you were to wish for something to begin, it would have to be to begin wrapping something up.

Please remember that Aries always comes after Pisces. All things end with Pisces and begin with Aries—that's the cycle of change in the Universe. In other words, Pisces is a sign of not only completion but also of preparation.

Before moving to the next stage, become the person who

can handle it. Let go of all physical and emotional baggage so that you can propel yourself forward a month later. When the New Moon or Full Moon is in Pisces, visualize your new self as you write your Power Wish.

Whatever happened in the past, forgive and accept all of it. The energy of Pisces is a forgiving heart that transmutes anger and hatred into gratitude.

If you are holding on to something that you haven't been able to forgive, how about giving it over to a Pisces Power Wish? A Pisces Full Moon Power Wish can gracefully end futile relationships that have been dragging on or have no future in sight.

Pisces is also deeply connected to healing. If you'd like to work and succeed in the healing arts, make a specific Power Wish with the New Moon in Pisces. Pisces Power Wishes can also be effective for those seeking a career in film, photography, art, dance, music, or other creative fields.

Pisces New Moon Power Wish

Late February to Late March

A Pisces New Moon helps you . . .

- ✦ Love and be loved
- ✦ Heal past hurts and traumas
- ✦ Have a big, loving heart and an open mind
- ✦ Receive power from the invisible
- ✦ Forgive someone you couldn't forgive before
- ✦ Circulate stagnant energy
- ✦ Manifest what you envision
- ✦ Master healing techniques or skills
- ✦ Allow your musical or artistic talent to blossom
- ✦ Bring closure to a dead-end relationship

✦ With anything related to the legs, lymphatic system, or sleep

Inquiries from the Universe

To help you find clues when you don't know what to write

✦ What is something that happened in the past that was traumatic for you?

✦ What is something you keep avoiding because you don't want to face it?

✦ What is something you become dependent on when under stress?

✦ What would you like to manifest with help from the invisible?

✦ What is the best life you can picture in your mind?

TOP 3 POWER WISH EXAMPLES THAT ARE LIKELY TO COME TRUE WITH A PISCES NEW MOON

1. <u>I intend for</u> everything I envision to become reality.
2. <u>I intend for</u> my love and talent to be used in the highest and best way for world peace.
3. <u>I intend to</u> connect with angels and spirit guides, receiving divine assistance.

RECOMMENDED KEYWORDS FOR PISCES POWER WISHES

🔑 *Love*

unconditional love, compassion, kindness, prayer, world peace, understanding, sympathy, empathy, assimilation, contribution, forgiveness

⚷ Healing

healer, spiritual, fantasy, envision, daydream, dream, the invisible, angel, spirit, tarot, oracle cards

⚷ Art

music, painting, computer graphics, 3-D, dance, photography, film

⚷ Water

scent, perfume, aroma, spirits, alcohol, ocean, beach, wave, swimming, surfing, yacht, water sports, spa, pool

⚷ Romantic

fantastical, magical, intuitive, unrealistic, imagined

⚷ Purify

cleanse, release, eliminate, pray, heal, take care of, accept, serve, cure, devote

ROMANTIC RELATIONSHIPS AND PARTNERSHIPS

- ✦ I intend for my future soul mate to appear in my dreams.
- ✦ I intend to forgive Kyle 100 percent, here and now, and move on to a new relationship with someone else.

CAREER AND BUSINESS

- ✦ I intend to tour the world as a crystal-singing-bowl player, healing people's hearts and souls.
- ✦ I intend to fully express all the dormant love inside me through my career.

FINANCES

- ✦ I intend for everything I envision to bring me money.
- ✦ I intend to attract money as naturally as breathing.

HABITS

- ✦ I intend to pick one spot every day and tidy up little by little.
- ✦ I intend to take watercolor classes, expressing the artistic talent that I've kept hidden.

PERSONALITY

+ I intend to let love guide my decisions, instead of judgment.

+ I intend to distance myself from complainers and hang out only with people who have good energy.

HEALTH AND BEAUTY

+ I intend to start swimming next month to get into the best possible shape.

+ I intend to drink at least eight glasses of water a day and build a healthy body that easily flushes out toxins.

MISCELLANEOUS

+ I intend to forgive anyone who's ever wronged me and elevate my whole life starting today.

+ I intend to keep praying with support from angels so that my father's illness is completely cured.

Pisces Full Moon Power Wish

Late August to Late September

The themes and keywords are the same as those for the New Moon. Additionally, a Pisces Full Moon helps you release . . .

- ✦ Carelessness, unhealthy lifestyles, addiction
- ✦ Cowardice, paranoia, dead-end relationships
- ✦ Troubles and worries about the legs; poor lymph circulation

TOP 2 POWER/RELEASE WISH
EXAMPLES THAT ARE LIKELY
TO COME TRUE WITH A PISCES
FULL MOON

1. The trauma I experienced from my parents is dis-appearing naturally. Now gratitude is all there is. Thank you so much, truly.
2. I let go of my unhealthy lifestyle. Now that I'm taking better care of myself, I've already lost seven pounds! Thank you so much.

ROMANTIC RELATIONSHIPS AND PARTNERSHIPS

✦ As soon as I got out of that dead-end relationship, I was introduced to a beautiful person. I see now that when you let go, new things really do come into your life. Thank you so much.

CAREER AND BUSINESS

✦ We started offering tarot readings at our salon, and now so many customers are coming back for more. Sales are soaring! Thank you so much.

FINANCES

✦ What I envisioned has become a reality and is bringing in a solid profit. It's amazing how the Universe works. Thank you so much.

HABITS

✦ Lately I'm no longer binge-eating, even when I'm feeling stressed out. It feels so much better to relieve stress by dancing. Thank you so much.

PERSONALITY

✦ Now that I have closure, I've been able to focus on myself and make my life so much better. My heart feels lighter now. Thank you so much.

HEALTH AND BEAUTY

◆ My metabolism has improved dramatically, thanks to the sea salt baths I've been taking. I'm now able to let go of all the negative emotions and stress of the day before I go to bed. Thank you so much!

MISCELLANEOUS

◆ Sending the energy of love and gratitude to my sister has erased all the grievances I was holding against her. I am now truly grateful that she is my sister, and my heart is at complete peace. Thank you so much.

PART 3

Getting More
Out of Your
Power Wish

Advanced Techniques for Fine-Tuning Your Power Wish

In the previous chapters, I explained the basics of the Power Wish Method. That method alone is perfectly sufficient, but I'm sure many people want to know about that trump card they can use when they really want a wish to come true. So for those of you who are interested, I'll go one step further and introduce some advanced Power Wishing techniques in this chapter. They are not required, but if you use them, your Power Wish will be even more effective. Think of them as the icing on the cake.

Techniques for a more effective Power Wish

1. Take full advantage of the New Moon and Full Moon occurring in your Moon sign (personal Moon sign Power Wish).
2. Review your Power Wishes during Mercury retrograde.
3. Add a Moon Collage to your Power Wish.
4. Receive the Universe's will with Moon Water.

I'll start with the first technique.

Technique 1

Take full advantage of the New Moon and
Full Moon occurring in your Moon sign
(personal Moon sign Power Wish).

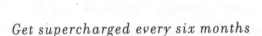

Get supercharged every six months
New Moons and Full Moons each occur twelve times a year,
but they occur in your own Moon sign only once. These oc-
currences are extremely special opportunities for not only a
Power Wish but also a "Miracle Wish" to come true.

As a reminder, what's popularly known as your "sign" in
horoscopes is actually your Sun sign. For example, if your
sign is Cancer, it means the Sun was positioned in Cancer
when you were born.

However, in astrology we use a total of ten celestial bodies, and the Sun is just one of them. Even if the Sun was in
Cancer, that doesn't necessarily mean the other nine celes-

tial bodies were also in Cancer. It's actually more likely that they were distributed among different signs.

One of those celestial bodies is the Moon. The Moon represents your essence, and in that sense, it's even more important than the Sun. Your personal Moon sign is the zodiac sign that the Moon was positioned in the moment you were born. When you start viewing your life through your Moon sign, you gain clarity and attract good fortune and opportunities one after another. It's not a coincidence that in Japanese, one of the words for fortune, *tsuki*, also means Moon.

You can look up your Moon sign at keikopowerwish.com.

Your Moon sign is the foundation of your life

I think the easiest way to understand the difference between the Sun sign and the Moon sign is to picture a tree. If the Sun sign is the trunk of the tree, the Moon sign would be the roots. Because the trunk is the visible part with a large surface area, it appears at first to be the star of the show. Yet what really makes the tree grow are the roots hidden beneath the ground. It's only because the roots spread out in all directions and absorb nutrients that the trunk can grow strong and wide.

The same goes for the Moon sign. It is from your Moon

sign that the tree of your life spreads its branches and leaves and bears flowers and fruit. It's not an exaggeration to say that whether your life can fully blossom depends on how well your Moon sign can "absorb nutrients."

The time for your Moon sign to absorb nutrients occurs twice a year, every six months. Specifically:

+ The day the New Moon occurs in your Moon sign (the personal Moon sign New Moon)
+ The day the Full Moon occurs in your Moon sign (the personal Moon sign Full Moon)

These two days are your ultimate supercharge days. On these days, all sixty trillion cells in your body voraciously absorb the Universal energy, like tree roots sending up nutrients from the ground. That is how you accumulate and store the ability to attract fortune.

When a New Moon or Full Moon occurs in your Moon sign . . .

Remember, a New Moon is a state in which the Moon and the Sun are perfectly aligned. And when the New Moon occurs in your Moon sign, the energy of the Moon and the Sun cascades straight toward you like an avalanche. Isn't it awesome just imagining this?

So then, what happens when the Full Moon occurs in your Moon sign? A Full Moon is a state in which the Moon and the Sun are facing each other. Even though the Moon and the Sun are positioned differently, they shower maximum energy on you, like a New Moon. The quality of the energy, however, will of course be different.

Whereas the New Moon is a time for beginnings, the Full Moon is a time for release. And when the Full Moon occurs in your Moon sign, it's no ordinary release; it is magnified to the level of purification.

All your mental shackles, including negative emotions, limiting beliefs, and traumas, are uprooted and completely removed. That is the kind of superpowerful detox that occurs along with the supercharge when the Full Moon is in your Moon sign.

Your Power Wish becomes a Miracle Wish

When the New Moon or Full Moon occurs in your Moon sign, the Universe's energy focuses on you. It's as if you have become an energy receiver. When the energy is focused, it means there's greater power to manifest your wish. In other words, your Power Wish is more likely to come true.

On these two occasions, it's actually possible for you to write a Miracle Wish. Even if your wish feels too far out of reach, there's a possibility it will come true against all odds when you write it as your Moon sign Power Wish. It could blow your mind. So when the New Moon or Full Moon occurs in your Moon sign, I recommend that you dare to write a wish that feels far-fetched.

For example, if in the other months you are comfortable wishing for an annual income of a hundred thousand dollars, how about writing this for your Moon sign Power Wish: "I intend for my annual income to exceed one million dollars."

If you had previously written "I intend to become Dylan's partner," perhaps you can try this for your Moon sign Power Wish: "I intend for Dylan to propose to me within one year, and that we'll be blessed with a baby soon after."

For your Moon sign Power Wish, unabashedly write things that you consider to be in the realm of dreams. The trick is to do it with a lighthearted attitude of "Ooh, maybe this really will come true!"—perhaps even hum your favorite tune while you write it.

Keep the Power Wish rules intact

For only your Moon sign Power Wish, you can ignore the sign's areas of expertise. Whether it's your desires, hopes, plans, thoughts, inspired ideas, dreams, or ideals, I recommend that you write everything and anything you'd like to see come true.

That said, make sure to follow the Power Wish rules. Although your wishes are more likely to come true, the way you write them still matters. I'd like you to follow the Power Wish rules properly, especially on your special days. You don't have to worry about the sign's themes, but don't forget the Anchoring Statements and Anchorings.

Use Power Words to raise the vibration even higher

Furthermore, I highly recommend incorporating Power Words (pages 60–61). As I've explained on pages 52–56, Power Words are words that can easily reach the Universe. They are high in vibration and help you plug into the Universe.

Try this: Read the words on pages 60–61 aloud. Don't you feel uplifted just by reading them? Don't you feel a sense of excitement coming over you? Don't they bring a smile to your face? That is the power of the Power Words. This feeling is the very essence of high vibration.

Reading them aloud makes it easier for you to feel their effect, but the vibration itself doesn't change when the words are only written, not spoken. When you incorporate Power Words into your Power Wish, your wish itself rises in vibration. Combined with the power of Anchoring Statements and Anchorings, your wish can now be delivered straight to the heart of the Universe.

Remember, when the New Moon or Full Moon is in your personal Moon sign, you are already plugged in to the Universe; it's a time when your wishes are especially likely to come true. If you add Power Words on top of all this, it will make you virtually unstoppable. Now the Universe can never ignore your wish!

That said, don't force Power Words into your wishes to the point where they start to sound awkward. Just use them whenever they feel like a good match for whatever you are wishing for—that's more than enough.

Personal Moon sign Power Wishes can be written within forty-eight hours

The essential rule of the Power Wish is to write it within ten hours (and if you can't do that, then within twenty-four hours at most) of the New Moon or Full Moon.

However, when the New Moon or Full Moon is occurring in your Moon sign, you can extend this time frame and write it within forty-eight hours. You can even write it two days in a row. That's because during these two occasions, the Universe's energy not only focuses on and pours over you, but it also stays with you longer.

Let the Universe decide which wish comes true first

On the days when the New Moon or Full Moon occurs in your Moon sign, not only do you receive a supercharge, but also the voice of your soul—your honest truth that is buried deep in your mind— may pop up and express itself. As a result, you may think of a wish that seems to come out of nowhere, or feel emotions that you've never felt before.

For example, you may have been planning in your head

to write a Power Wish about becoming the top seller in the department and getting promoted, but as soon as you sit down to write it, you realize that what you really want is to enjoy a relaxing life by the beach. Sometimes it may seem like you have a whole list of wishes that contradict one another, and that's okay. Even if you have two wishes that you don't think can come true at the same time, don't worry about it—just be honest and write them both down.

In your Moon sign Power Wish, pull out all the stops and tell the Universe everything you really want. And then let the Universe grant your wishes one by one, starting with the ones that are easiest to manifest.

PERSONAL MOON SIGN POWER WISH REVIEW

Write your Power Wish within forty-eight hours. You can even write it two days in a row.

Incorporate Power Words. (See pages 60–61.)

Write down whatever comes to mind, regardless of the sign's areas of expertise.

Don't forget to use the Anchoring Statements and Anchorings.

Technique 2

Review your Power Wishes during Mercury retrograde.

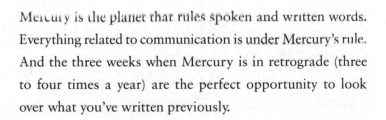

Mercury is the planet that rules spoken and written words. Everything related to communication is under Mercury's rule. And the three weeks when Mercury is in retrograde (three to four times a year) are the perfect opportunity to look over what you've written previously.

What is Mercury retrograde?

"Mercury retrograde" has become such a buzzword these days; even people who know nothing about astrology have heard of it. Perhaps you become anxious at the mention of it—after all, there are certain things to watch out for when Mercury is in retrograde. However, not all aspects of Mercury retrograde are negative. In fact, as long as we fully understand its nature, it can be a powerful tool.

Mercury retrograde is not to be feared but to be taken advantage of.

Retrograde is a phenomenon in which a planet appears to be moving backward. It is not actually moving backward, but due to its position relative to Earth, as both planets revolve around the Sun, it appears as if it is sliding back. You know how when you pass a car on the highway, it looks as if the car is gradually sliding backward? It's the same thing.

It's not just Mercury that goes into retrograde. Aside from the Moon and the Sun, all the planets used in astrology (Mercury, Venus, Mars, Jupiter, Saturn, Uranus, Neptune, Pluto) go into retrograde. So why is Mercury retrograde the only one that's talked about?

There are two reasons:

1. TANGIBLE EFFECTS

Mercury is the planet that governs not only words but also information (electronic devices), communication, and transportation. Since all of these are closely tied to our everyday lives, the effect of Mercury retrograde is easily recognized.

Examples: smartphone breaking, computer freezing, losing phone signals, emails getting lost (or getting sent by mistake), misunderstandings, no replies, traffic jams or accidents, flight delays, being late, etc.

2. PROXIMITY TO EARTH

On average, Mercury is the planet closest to Earth (the Moon is closest to Earth, followed by Mercury), so we can feel its effects more strongly. We don't really care what someone out in the distance is doing, but if someone nearby makes a funny move, it alarms us. It's the same thing.

When you read the first reason, it does sound troubling,

but everything has positive and negative sides. When Mercury is in retrograde, things do slow down, but the good news is that it's actually the perfect time for reviewing, retrying, and working on solidifying foundations. Retrograde is a time to look back. If you are currently studying something, start reviewing the material when the retrograde begins. That way, what you learn will stick, and you can master the subject more quickly.

The same goes for a Power Wish. When you take a second look at the Power Wishes you've previously written, they are imprinted deeper in your subconscious, and as a result, your wishes can come true more easily. This is because manifesting is a collaboration between the Universe and your subconscious mind.

Use reviewing to anchor yourself deeper in the Universe

When Mercury is in retrograde, it is a time for reinforcement. Think of it as an opportunity to anchor yourself deeper in the Universe.

RECOMMENDED PRACTICES DURING MERCURY RETROGRADE

Read over the Power Wishes you've previously written (it's better to read them aloud).

Revise or modify the Power Wishes you've previously written.

As you read over your Power Wishes, visualize them in your mind.

In a notebook, make a collage of images (such as magazine cutouts) that represent what you wrote (Moon Collage).

It would be ideal if you could do all four of these, but if that's too difficult, then make the last item, the Moon Collage, your top priority. I'll explain this soon, but making Moon Collages during Mercury retrograde is amazingly powerful!

Our logical, thinking mind (the left side of the brain)

tends to become a little dull when Mercury is in retrograde. However, this is actually an advantage for making a Moon Collage, which involves the right side of the brain, because you can use your right brain without the left brain getting in the way. Mercury retrograde is also the perfect time to practice visualization.

MERCURY RETROGRADE SCHEDULE

2020: February 18–March 9 / June 17–July 12 / October 13–November 3

2021: January 30–February 20 / May 29–June 22 / September 27–October 18

2022: January 14–February 3 / May 10–June 2 / September 9–October 2 / December 29–January 18, 2023

For an extended schedule, visit keikopowerwish.com.

Technique 3

Add a Moon Collage to your Power Wish.

Power Wish on one side of the spread;
Moon Collage on the facing side

If you want your Power Wishes to fully come true, I recommend you use a special notebook for them. The trick is to use each two-page spread to link your Power Wish to inspirational images. All you have to do is (1) write your Power Wish on one page (either on the left or right is fine), and then (2) on the opposite page, paste images that represent the wish. Simply flip through a magazine and pick out images that are a perfect match for your Power Wish. When you come across one that speaks to you, cut it out and add it to your notebook. You can also browse images on the internet and print them out, of course. It's a very fun exercise.

As you may recall, I originally came up with the Moon

Collage technique when my friend Wakako told me she was "terrible at visualizing" (see page 22), and I asked myself what she could do instead. Wakako herself is proof that Moon Collages are just as effective as visualization.

You can do both (1) and (2) at the same time on the New Moon and Full Moon. You can also take the time-lapse approach and do only (1) on the New Moon and Full Moon and then do (2) during Mercury retrograde. There are no set rules around this, so feel free to do what you like. What's important here is to have fun!

The Moon Collage technique is very popular in my circle. One of my friends is so into it that she uses up a whole notebook just for her personal Moon sign Power Wishes every year. More than 90 percent of the wishes she has written in her notebooks have come true! That's the strength of the Power Wish Method. It's a testament to how effective it can be to dedicate a notebook to the Power Wish/Moon Collage combination.

Communicating with the Universe in a way it can easily understand

There are two reasons why you need a Moon Collage.

First, it communicates easily with the Universe. You know the saying "Seeing is believing"? Rather than trying to describe, for instance, a moth orchid to someone with words—"It's a white flower, shaped like a butterfly, but not pointy"—you could just show them a photo of the flower, and they'd get it so much faster.

The same goes for the Universe. Even though a Power Wish remains the best way to connect to the Universe, imagery goes a long way toward helping the Universe understand it. If the Universe can understand your wishes more easily, then your wishes are that much more likely to come true.

The timing at which the Universe sends you signs
The other reason for making a Moon Collage is that it helps you recognize signs from the Universe. This is because the process stimulates the right side of the brain.

It's the Universe's job to create opportunities and synchronicity. We should leave this entirely to the Universe. On the other hand, it is our job to catch all these opportunities.

Especially during the first few days after you write a Power Wish, the Universe will send you signs frequently. If you are able to recognize these signs, your wish is as good as fulfilled. The entire process of the Power Wish Method starts with you writing your wish and ends with you recognizing the signs from the Universe.

But the reality is that some people ignore the opportunities the Universe creates for them, and some can't even recognize the signs to begin with. The Universe is sending them clear signs, and yet so many people are lamenting that they have no opportunities or encounters!

The reason why you miss the signs from the Universe

Why don't these people recognize the signs from the Universe? Or rather, why can't they? It's because they don't have their antenna up—the antenna to catch the signals from the Universe.

This antenna is connected to the right side of the brain, so the more you activate the right brain, the easier it will become for you to catch the signals. You'll also begin to experience one synchronicity after another.

Yet, in our current society, we can't help but be left-brain-oriented. Unless we consciously create opportunities to use the right brain, it will remain asleep for most of us. This is why so many people don't even notice the signs that the Universe is patiently sending them.

So you used this highly effective technique known as the Power Wish Method, and your wish reached the Universe. But if you can't recognize the signs from the Universe, it's as though you don't have the tools to reap the delicious fruit from the seeds you planted. What a waste!

You have just been introduced to the secret art of the

Power Wish. You learned the most powerful way to make your wish come true. Now you also have to learn to recognize the signs from the Universe. This is why I recommend using Moon Collages.

Technique 4

Receive the Universe's will with Moon Water.

A wish comes true when two parties share the same will. For example, a couple can get married only when they share the will to do so.

The best-case scenario, of course, is for your will to match the Universe's. When this happens, any and all of your wishes come true, no matter how outrageous or ambitious they may seem.

The Universe's will is consistently revealed on the New Moon and Full Moon. So if you decipher the Universe's will from a star chart and write a Power Wish that aligns with it, the likelihood of your wish coming true is close to 100 percent. That's the big secret.

But that's difficult, isn't it? Unless you are a master astrologer, it's difficult to decipher the Universe's will from a star chart. So what can we do? Is there any way to learn what the Universe wills, aside from reading the stars?

Oh, yes. There is a way to learn the Universe's will without bothering with star charts. Well, to be more accurate, with this method you don't "learn" the Universe's will so much as you naturally sync up with it.

And that method is to make Moon Water and drink it.

For those of you who have never heard of it, Moon Water is water that you expose to the energy of the Moon for more than two hours during the New Moon or Full Moon. When you drink this water and absorb the vibration of the Universe into your body, you essentially take in the Universe's will.

The Universe's will is really a vibration that holds all of its thoughts and intentions. We use words to show our intentions, but the Universe expresses them all with its vibration. This vibration itself is the Universe's will.

Water records vibrations

It's a well-known fact that water records vibrations. For example, there is a study showing that water exposed to the words *thank you* formed very different crystals than water exposed to the words *you idiot*. Another study showed a similar result with water exposed to the music of Mozart versus water exposed to heavy metal music.*

As these studies tell us, water accurately understands, absorbs, and records information it is given. Moon Water utilizes this very characteristic of water. Water bathed in moonlight during the New Moon is called New Moon Water, and water bathed in moonlight during the Full Moon is called Full Moon Water.

What's wonderful about Moon Water is that it allows us to absorb the energy of the Moon into our bodies through water, a substance that is essential to us. It delivers the energy of the Moon and the Universe to all sixty trillion of our cells. Isn't that amazing?

---

*Masuru Emoto, *The Hidden Messages in Water* (New York: Atria, 2005).

Power Wish works with the mind;
Moon Water works with the body

Our physical body and our mind make a pair. When both of them move in the same direction, we feel balanced in our life and in our being, and everything starts to fall into place.

The Power Wish Method works with the mind through words and imagery. How about the body? If the mind and the body have to move in the same direction in order for our wish to come true, we also need to tell our body about our Power Wish by drinking Moon Water.

Please remember that the part of you that takes action to bring your wish to life is not your mind but your body—all sixty trillion of your cells, to be precise.

This being the case, you also need your cells to understand your wish. When your mind and body are aligned, your wish can become a reality.

How to use Moon Water to boost your Power Wish

A. Let the Moon Water record your Power Wish

This is super easy. Write your Power Wish in your designated notebook, place a blue glass bottle of water on top of that page, and leave it in the moonlight for at least two hours—that's it! If you have already created a Moon Collage at this point, you can also place another bottle on top of the collage and let it soak in the energy of the Moon.

Please note, it's crucial that the bottle be blue and made of glass. Blue is the color that is most effective in attracting the Moon's vibration, and glass is the material that is most compatible with its vibration. Don't use plastic bottles—they block the vibration of the Moon. Water will not turn into Moon Water in a plastic bottle, even if you leave it under the Moon.

During the two hours when the bottle of water is exposed to the moonlight, the water in the bottle absorbs and records the vibration of your Power Wish. All you need to do is drink the Moon Water once it's ready. Your cells receive the "order"—your Power Wish—and will work as one to attract the reality that you, their master, desire.

B. Write your Power Wish while drinking Moon Water

With method A, you let Moon Water record your Power Wish, which means you'll need to have finished writing your Power Wish before you make the Moon Water. However, there's another way that reverses the process, and it's just as powerful.

With this method, even though the Moon Water will not record your Power Wish, you will be writing it while being supported by the vibration of the New Moon or Full Moon that is recorded in the Moon Water. And the effect is immediate! It's as if the Universe is standing by your side with a bar code scanner, entering your wish into its system as soon as you write it. That's the kind of partnership with the Universe that you can expect.

Both A and B work equally well; one is not better than the other. Do whichever is easier or feels right to you at the time.

Events do unfold according to the zodiac sign
New Moon Water and Full Moon Water record not only the information from your Power Wish. They also record the information from the zodiac sign that the New Moon or Full Moon is occurring in, and attract the reality that aligns with it.

I myself have been drinking Moon Water for God knows how many decades. From my years of experience, I know that each zodiac sign produces Moon Water that is unique in taste and texture. Furthermore, the events that unfold and the people you meet after you drink it also vary according to the sign.

For example, the Moon Water you make with the New Moon or Full Moon in Taurus is quite rich. It's thick and has a full-bodied flavor. And after I drink it, I often receive delicious gifts (such as a limited-edition Swiss roll cake from a famous pastry shop that someone had bought too many of), get invited to dinner by a foodie, or receive tickets to an art exhibition.

On the other hand, the Moon Water you make with the New Moon or Full Moon in Sagittarius is light and doesn't have much flavor. Even when I make it on a cold day, it feels ever so slightly lukewarm for some reason. What's interesting is that as soon as I drink it, I start getting emails from overseas! In my case, it's partially because I already have more international connections than most people, but even so, it's fascinating to get a burst of international communication whenever I drink Sagittarius Moon Water. Sometimes I even get booked for an unexpected international business trip the day after drinking it.

All events materialize from vibration

If you drink Moon Water for a while, I think you will also start to frequently experience events that are related to the zodiac sign of the Moon Water. This is because the Moon Water recorded the energy of the sign, and that information was transmitted to the cells of your body when you drank it.

Everything that happens in this world is a projection of your own energy. Perhaps you drank Moon Water of Cancer—which has a deep connection to the home—and found the perfect apartment. Or you drank Moon Water of Libra—which represents partnership—and was asked out on a date by someone you're interested in. None of these are coincidences. As far as I'm concerned, they are simply consequences. That's how vibration works.

The vibration of the Moon attracts fortune

As a personal hobby, I've been experimenting for years with recording the vibration of the Moon onto everyday items ("attunement"). What I've found is that liquids such as water and oil (100 percent organic only) are best for absorbing and recording the vibration of the Moon, especially water. Because our bodies are 70 percent water, they absorb Moon Water with no resistance whatsoever. In other words, the vibration of Moon Water becomes a part of you.

If you regularly drink Moon Water twice a month, it's only natural that you will start beating to the rhythm of the Moon and eventually the Universe. You will also have better fortune, of course. As I mentioned before, the word *tsuki* in Japanese means both "fortune" and "Moon." It is the Moon—with its fast orbit and rapidly shifting aspects with other celestial bodies—that creates the events and windows of opportunity we call "fortune" or "luck."

How to make and use Moon Water

Lastly, let me go over how to make Moon Water, although it's very easy. On the night of a New Moon or Full Moon, pour spring or filtered water (any brand; not carbonated) into a blue glass bottle (preferably larger than a wine bottle) and let it sit under the Moon for more than two hours. The best location to place the bottle is in the yard or on the porch. The windowsill is fine, too.

Sometimes I receive emails that say, "I couldn't make Moon Water last night because of the rain," but you can still make Moon Water when it's cloudy, raining, or snowing. This is because the power of the Moon does not change, whether we can see it or not. Think about it: You can't see the Moon on the New Moon to begin with. Please keep this in mind.

Once you make Moon Water, drink it all within forty-eight hours. It is best, though, if you drink it sooner. I usually drink it all within one hour.

Moon Water is alive, just like perishable food. As time passes, the vibration of the Moon escapes. If you made too much to drink, you can add it to your bath or use it to wash your face or hair.

I also recommend placing a glass of it by your bedside. When we sleep at night, our energy is restored and our cells are repaired. This is also when our fortune accumulates. In Japan we have a saying: "A child who sleeps grows"; the same is true for fortune.

That said, negative energy is also drawn to us at night, so we need to put up a good shield. Purifying your bedroom twice a month using New Moon Water and Full Moon Water, which have high purification power, can be a powerful way to keep negative energy away. All you need to do is place the water by your bedside. Be sure to discard it the following morning without drinking it.

HOW TO MAKE MOON WATER

WHAT YOU'LL NEED

1. A blue glass bottle (Don't use plastic bottles—they block the vibration of the Moon. Be aware that water will not turn into New Moon Water or Full Moon Water in a plastic bottle, even if you leave it under the Moon.)
2. Spring or filtered water (any brand; not carbonated)

PREPARATION

1. Pour the spring water into the blue glass bottle, then close the cap.
2. Let it sit under the Moon for at least two hours.
3. If you want the Moon Water to record your Power Wish, open your Power Wish notebook and place the bottle on top of your writing or your inspirational images before you let it sit in the moonlight.

Want to Know More About Power Wish?

Visit keikopowerwish.com to:

✦ View the full calendar of New Moons and Full
  Moons.
✦ Look up your personal Moon sign.
✦ Find out when Mercury goes into retrograde.